THE DONUT TREE
BY TONY MANN

I dedicate this book to my friend Doug.

Table of Contents

Introduction

An introduction is supposed to explain what the reader of a book can expect to learn. An introduction in a teaching book should also explain how the book is organized.

First, this book is a practical guide to help persons with mental illness to have good lives. Also, it helps families and supporters to help those persons have good lives.

The book is in two parts. Part One will go over the following page which can be made into a card to carry around. The card highlights the most important parts of the book and was developed through two years of daily talking group sessions with patients who had been in and out of hospital and/or jail many times. I and patients in group felt we needed a simple plan that would work and could be referred to in the moment. Part One is about how to put the following card into action.

Goal 1: Get Out.
Goal 2: Stay Out.

How?
Make your behavior match your goal.

Frustration:
Have a plan to deal with frustration so that frustration will lead to Social Cooperation and not Social Confrontation.

Best Trick I Know:
Be in the right place at the right time, because all the times that you are in the right place at the right time you cannot be in the wrong place at the wrong time.

All parts in Part One are interrelated but the main subject of each chapter will be highlighted. The group leader's words (my words!) are italicized to make it easy to read.

Part Two will discuss:

• Freedom and responsibility.
• Nutrition.
• Three over-the-counter supplements I feel all persons with mental illness should be taking, how they should be taking them and why they should be taking them.
• Why it is so hard for persons with mental illness to quit smoking.

Any resemblance to persons living or dead is strictly coincidental.

PART ONE

1   *May I have some gum?*

Goal 1: Get Out. Goal 2: Stay Out.

Greg P. was, and I hope still is, a 50-something-year-old chronic schizophrenic patient taking two different anti-psychotics and a mood stabilizer along with other medicines to fight high cholesterol and high blood pressure. When I met Greg I was the medical provider for a chronic 34-bed mental hospital unit. My role as a Family Nurse Practitioner was to sit in the doctor's chair in the treatment team and make decisions about which medicines would best help our patients both medically and psychiatrically.

Greg had been at a forensic psychiatric hospital but the charges against him were nol-prossed (the charges were dropped) and he was transferred to our unit. A forensic psychiatric hospital is simply a place where mentally ill people are sent when they have violated some law and are thought to be too dangerous to be treated outside of a hospital or their crime was serious enough that if they were not mentally ill they would have been put in jail or prison. The nursing staff had informed me that he had, in fact, been taken out of seclusion to be sent to our unit.

Seclusion is somewhat like solitary confinement in a prison but is supposed to be used only when someone's behavior is so out of control that the patient needs to be separated from the other patients. Unlike solitary confinement, it is not supposed to be used as a punishment for behavior; when a patient can control his behavior, the patient has to be let out of seclusion.

Over the first month or so that Greg was with us, he was repeat-edly in seclusion for 'attacking staff.' This was always during the late afternoon or night shifts and I had never seen his behavior first hand. In the mornings when I arrived he was always friendly and cooperative with me, so I let him out of seclusion, usually even before morning report.

Morning report is when nighttime staff tells the oncoming day shift what happened during the night.

As I said earlier, I had never seen Greg attack staff until late one morning…

The unit was having a lunch for staff and all staff were to cook something and bring it from home. As a football fan, I had long experience making really good chicken wings (or so I like to think.) Just before the lunch was to start, I was walking down a hall alone with a pan full of chicken wings when I was approached by Greg who was waving his arms in a threatening way with his fists balled up. Greg was a big man, 6'3" and not slight. He was also once a good-looking man, resembling John Wayne before the ravages of mental illness had taken its toll. But where Greg is 6'3", I'm almost 6'5" and not physically shy with my body as I both mountain bike and whitewater kayak. Instead of dropping my chicken wings, I turned my back to Greg to protect the wings. Greg then started striking my back multiple times. I was now experiencing how Greg attacked staff. Even though Greg was a large man and could have hit me very hard, he was actually hitting me with very light taps. He obviously was not trying to hurt me. Other staff then came to my call and took control of Greg, and I took my wings to a safe area and went back to find out what was going on with Greg. Now Greg is very child-like in his demeanor (how he speaks with others) and, when I asked him why he decided to hit me, Greg said, "I'm nervous."

After a little further questioning I began to understand that Greg was trying to get a shot of Ativan so that he wouldn't be nervous. Ativan is regularly used for behavioral management PRNs (PRN meaning "as needed") per protocol by the hospital where I was working.

I negotiated with Greg to stop pseudo-attacking (pretend attacking) staff and to just ask for a PRN when he felt he needed one. I also told him he could have 2 PRNs a day. Greg agreed and, as I was chewing gum, Greg asked if he could have a piece of gum. I gave him a piece of gum.

A week or two went by and Greg was now asking for PRNs instead of "attacking staff" to get PRNs. I negotiated again with Greg to take PRNs by mouth (take a pill) rather than getting a shot. Greg agreed and again asked for a piece of gum. I gave him a piece to kind of "seal the deal," I suppose. Later that day Greg asked for a PRN and came back in 10 minutes or so and said, "It's not working," and I told him to wait. By mouth medicine (by mouth is called "PO") takes longer to work than "IM" (IM means an intra-muscular shot). He was satisfied with this and asked for another piece of gum. I pointed out that he was still chewing the one I had given him earlier. I didn't give him one then, but as I thought about the previous episodes, I thought about how behavior, all behavior, is goal-driven.

Greg had "attacked staff" not because he wanted to hurt anyone but because he felt nervous and knew he would get a shot so he used a behavior to meet his goal. The problem of course was he would never get out of the hospital as long as he used that approach. Once I figured out the goal of his behavior, we easily changed his behavior to be more appropriate or "convergent" with society's expectations for behavior. Now that we had changed the behavior, I wondered if we could further change the means of Greg reaching his goal of not being nervous?

I went back to Greg and asked what if, instead of getting Ativan PO when he was nervous, he got a piece of gum instead. He could still have the Ativan later, but "let's first try a piece of gum." Greg liked gum, so he agreed. We put gum in the medicine cart for Greg, using his own funds to restock it once a month. He rarely, if ever, received Ativan PRN after that and was eventually placed in a group home. What's the point? There actually are several.

Divergent behavior is what gets mentally ill persons in trouble with greater society. So what is "divergent"? And who is society? First, society really is just the people around you and their expectations for others' behavior.

Divergent just means a behavior away from what is expected in the situation where the behavior occurs. For example, a person does something that makes others wonder if the person is okay or mentally ill. Jumping up and screaming when your team makes a touchdown in a football game is not divergent, it's convergent; that is, it is convergent with what other fans would be doing. Jumping up and screaming in the middle of the street is divergent from what other people expect, so people wonder what is wrong, has something happened? Was someone hurt? And if there is no obvious reason for the person to be jumping up and down and screaming in the middle of the street, others will wonder if there is something wrong with the way the person is thinking or perceiving the world.

Now the person jumping up and down and screaming in the middle of the street for no apparent reason does have a goal. It just isn't easy to understand what the goal of the behavior is, so the behavior is divergent just as Greg hitting staff was divergent. He had a goal, but the goal was not to hurt staff. He had an understandable goal but used the wrong behavior to obtain his goal.

His goal was to not be nervous and his behavior was in line with his goal, but the behavior he used to reach his goal was divergent from society's rules. You cannot hit someone to get what you want.

The points? Behavior is always goal-driven. The question is whether the behavior is convergent (acceptable to society and those around you) or divergent (not acceptable to society and those around you). Also, is the behavior congruent with your goal? Congruent just means "in line with what you want." Greg's behavior in hitting staff was congruent with his goal of getting a shot but divergent in that it is not acceptable to society. He would never get out of the hospital behaving like that. Asking for a PRN was congruent with his goal and his behavior then was also convergent with society's expectations of behavior. He could now get out of the hospital and go to a group home.

So we have three new words regarding behavior:
- Congruent: Is the behavior in line with your goal?
- Convergent: Is the behavior acceptable to society in the situation the behavior is found?
- Divergent: Is the behavior unacceptable to society in the situation the behavior is found?

To be successful in reaching our goals, our behavior needs to be congruent with our goals and our behavior needs to also be convergent with the community standards of where we live. As long as our behavior is both congruent and convergent, we will likely not find ourselves in a jail or a hospital.

It is very important to understand that ALL behavior is goal-driven. Having said that, we must make our behavior match our goals in ways that are acceptable to the rules of society.

So how do we make our behavior both congruent (in line) with what we want and convergent with society's rules?

We will begin to cover the "how" in the next section, but first the reader should review and reread the previous section, as much of the information needed to survive mental illness and have a good life is contained in the section just read. Think about how Greg's goal to not be nervous was an acceptable goal but the way he went about reaching his goal was unacceptable and would prevent him from getting out of the hospital. You cannot use force or violence to have your needs met.

You also must have goal/behavior congruence. Your behavior must be in line with your goal and your behavior needs to be acceptable. For example, cooperating with staff would help you get out of the hospital. Yelling and demanding that staff let you out would have the opposite effect. Angry demanding behavior would tend to keep you in the hospital, so yelling at others would not be in line or congruent with reaching your goal of getting out of the hospital.

The next section will begin teaching simple, practical ways to help manage your life in the real-world situation of being in the hospital (a closed environment), then getting out and living successfully in a more open environment. But first: what are open and closed environments?

Define "open and closed environment."
A closed environment is like a lockdown hospital unit or a jail or prison. Jails and prisons are meant to contain and punish dangerous people, and to protect the public from those dangerous people.

A lockdown hospital is meant to protect the patient and to limit outside stimulation to significantly cut down environmental stress.

An open environment has much more environmental stress and has many more choices to be made.

What is environmental stress?
All the choices we all have to make daily in an open environment contribute to environmental stress. We have to decide where we eat, what we eat, how we get something to eat and where we sleep. Whom do we choose to be around; how do we pay our bills? How do we get to the doctor, to the store? What medicines are we supposed to take and what dose, what amount and at what

time? How do we get our medicines? How will we pay for them? All of these and more are stressors that we experience in an open environment.

A therapeutic or healing closed environment greatly reduces these pressures. We don't have to worry about getting something to eat, something to drink or where and when to sleep. We are given our medicines at the right time and in the right amounts. The stresses related to making daily decisions are greatly reduced. This is because those decisions are being made for us.

2   Make your behavior match your goal
   (Goal/behavior congruence)

So you are in the hospital and they say you need treatment and that you are mentally ill. What should you do?

The first thing to do is to identify your primary GOAL.

Or, said another way, what is it you most want?

Most patients in your situation will identify their GOAL as being:

Get out. As soon as possible.

So goal number one for most people would be to "GET OUT."

The second goal most patients in your situation will agree to is: "Once out, STAY OUT."

So...

Goal 1: Get out.

Goal 2: Stay out.

How are these goals to be accomplished? First you must understand that what gets persons admitted to inpatient mental hospitals is not what they think or how they think.

Let's repeat that because it is VERY important. Do you hear voices? There is no law against that. There is no law against having unusual ideas, thoughts or beliefs. How you think or what you believe probably did not get you put in the hospital.

It's a person's BEHAVIOR that gets them admitted.

Let's look at the following example. Two people hear voices and both believe the voices they hear are from a powerful supernatural being such as God.

The voices tell both people to hit another person. One person does what the voices say and one person does not. Which person is more likely to get into trouble and be put in jail or in the hospital?

That's right, the person who listened to the voices and hit the other person is the one who gets in trouble. His behavior violated the community standards and hearing voices does not excuse the behavior. You may not go to jail or you may not stay in jail but if your behavior hurts other people in the community then your freedom to do what you want will be limited. If you are not locked up in jail you will likely be locked up in a hospital.

Thoughts or beliefs do not get people in trouble; actions do.

Behavior gets you in trouble — not the voices or the ideas. So we must learn to MAINTAIN our behavior so that we don't get into trouble with those people around us. Medicines can help but just taking meds will not cause us to have a good life.

So how do we learn to maintain our behavior?

It's actually easier than you might think. First we make goals, then we learn to match our behavior to our goals.

And the trick of surviving mental illness is to set goals, make your behavior match your goals and make sure that your behavior is in line or convergent with community standards. Any medicines you take for mental illness should make it easier to keep your behavior convergent with community standards while also being congruent or in line with your goals.

So to review:

Goal 1. Get Out.

Goal 2. Stay Out.

How?

Make your behavior match your goal.

Group Discussion: Make your behavior match your goal.

(Group leader's words are in italics, not in quote marks.)
Behavior fact: when we talk about "make your behavior match your goal" that sounds easy but what does it mean? What do we know about behavior? Well, one thing that I would point out is "What you do today you tend to do tomorrow."[Writing on board]

Did I spell tomorrow right?

Curt J: "That's close enough."

What you do today you tend to do tomorrow. Another way that people say that, a popular phrase for saying it…

The best predictor of future performance is your past behavior. What you have done in the past, you will tend to do in the future. So, if somebody tends to get out and goes back to using drugs and alcohol or tends not to show up on time, whatever they tended to do before they tend to do it in the future. Unless some kind of change happens.

So, what you do today you will tend to do tomorrow. What are some other behavior facts?

Thomas: "Um, being assertive and aggressive. You could be assertive for today and then you could be assertive for tomorrow but you still got that the influence in you to go out there because you are having symptoms. You know them symptoms could attract you the behavior in your mind and if you ain't careful enough it could lead to symptoms of going back and drinking."

Well, okay, let's try this. Let me ask you a question. Is it illegal to hear voices?

Group: "No."

Is it illegal to have unusual beliefs or delusions?

Group: "No."

Curt J: "Yeah."

No, it's not illegal. So what gets people who hear voices or believe unusual things, what is it that gets them in trouble?

Curt J: "Their behavior."

So really everything is behavior-driven, right? Everything is behavior-driven. People... you can talk to yourself, you can hear voices, as long as you do not do anything that attracts attention or upsets people... what is it... society has this legal thing and it is pretty much the same, worded a little bit differently in all states but it is always the same basic idea, it's when your behavior gets to the point that they think you are "dangerous to yourself and/or others." Dangerous to yourself and/or others. And then they throw this into it — it's not "IS," it's "MAY BE." So the legal system gives itself a hedge, they get to hedge their bets a little bit. It's not that, "We know that you ARE," because the only way that you know someone IS dangerous to themselves or others is if they have done something dangerous to themselves or others, right? Somebody goes out and shoots up a bunch of people in a store just for the heck of it; pretty sure that person is dangerous to other people. Then they shoot themselves in the foot or the head, well, now we know that they are dangerous to themselves. Right? But you want to catch people before it gets to that point, right? Society has an interest in catching that before something unfixable happens. So, "Oh, they are doing some things, doing some things that we don't understand what they are doing," a person is saying some different kind of things, doing some different kind of things, so we think "MAY BE," they may be dangerous to themselves or others.

Curt J: "Well I got, sometimes we may have a case. Against the state. I do."

Thomas: "I feel like if you making more problems for yourself I feel like you could actually feel dangerous to yourself you could actually feel that increase be more dangerous to yourself that what you are supposed to be assertive for."

Learn to manage your own behavior.

Curt J: "I had some bad doctors."

Or others will manage it for you, Curt.

Is this true? Learn to manage your own behavior or others will manage it for you.

Thomas: "Yeah."

That… this, this is one of those kind of things that you read and go, "Ouch, that hurts." That's a big ouch, right? You have got to learn to manage your own behavior or other people are going to be managing it for you.

Curt J: "Especially my family that sent me down to Atlanta, so…"

Thomas: "So the problem is to get out, stay out. Why do you want to get out, just because you want to get out to drink alcohol? You want to get out because you want to drink a beer or you want to get out because you want to drink wine. You stay out it means that you are not drinking beer, you are not drinking wine, you are not using street drugs. You think you going to get out and use street drugs and, and stay out, it is not going to happen."

Right, that's right. That made sense. Let's give him a hand. It was short, it didn't wander and it was concise. It was short and it made sense; it was good.

Ralph: "It was good."

That's what I'm saying. Sometimes people are like, "What is he talking about?" You try to use words that are too big, well, we all do, but say things simply, directly and not wander around. Have a thought, complete the thought and then have another thought. But don't, don't... you have a problem, you don't complete your thought before you move onto another thought. So you need to have one simple thought at a time, not saying that you are simple-minded. I'm saying that is what we all need to do because I do the same thing. I'll start off and I'll be going here and going there, and I'll be like, "What was I talking about? Does anybody know? I don't know."

Oh yeah, behavior. Get out and stay out. The way you get out is you make your behavior in here such that they say, "Oh, they can get out. They are doing a good job in here, they are doing everything in here that we want them to do." People who come in and fight the system and say, "Well, I'm not going to let you tell me what to do," they don't get out as fast. Right? It's the people who come in and say, "Yeah, I have got things I have to deal with..." You don't have to agree with everything in here; everybody has their own mind. You don't have to agree with everything, but you do have to understand that "I'm here and somewhere down the road somebody thought I might be dangerous to myself and/or others" or, if you are in the judicial kind of part of it, the Criminal Psychiatric Hospital part of it, you HAVE done something because forensics... there has been something that has happened negative that society has a vested interest in trying to have not happen again.

Thomas: "So I know what that is."

What is that?

Thomas: "I was driving my car up to my apartment and the police stopped me and I had a beer in the car and he asked me if I needed any help and I told him no. I was stopping, parking my car because I ran out of gas. And he asked me for identification. I told him, right now I'm having a problem with my car and he still asked me for my identification. And I said, "No, I don't have identification." And he locked me up."

Yeah, you are not supposed to drive a car without having identification. And I will tell you, I will tell you, everybody here, it makes the police angry if you don't have identification on you. Always have, if you don't have a driver's license, get one of those picture IDs, in fact I think the social workers get people those kind of picture IDs before they get out don't they?

Thomas: "Yeah, they do."

Jeff: "They used to do it."

Yeah, I know they used to do it. I think they still do. And the reason is because police, you know, people look at the police… people are fearful of the police and certainly things have happened at the police's hands that are not very nice. Right, but the police, on the flip side, they don't know when they go out to work if they are coming home that night. You know they just had some idiot kid got in an argument with his mom and he killed three cops that showed up at his house because the dog peed on the floor. That, that may be dangerous to yourself or others. Think about that. You got a guy, 22 years old, gets in a fight with his mom because the DOG peed on the carpet, peed on the floor. So she calls the cops and he gets out a gun and kills three cops. If that isn't senseless…

Thomas: "He killed his mom?"

No, he killed three cops. They just showed up to the door because she called them because the dog peed on the, well, not because the dog peed on the carpet but because they got into an argument.

Thomas: "Was he mentally ill?"

I don't know. But there was something wrong with him.

Thomas: "I think he must of been mentally ill, to do something like that."

It definitely was not good judgment. I mean he has killed three people, now there are three families that don't have fathers or sons and…

Thomas: "That's probably why people don't want to let us out, because of all that killing and stuff that is going on."

I mean there is no understanding it. There is no good reason for any of that to happen.

Curt J: "No reasoning."

Families fight...

Thomas: "Did she call the police on him?"

I haven't heard that much of it; I'm guessing that is what happened.

Thomas: "She must of called the police on him. She had to call the police on him, not the dog. She called the police on him."

Yeah.

Thomas: "Yeah, she called the police on him."

Probably, probably. That's what I'm saying is that society has a vested interest in not having that kind of stuff happen. So what I was talking about, the picture IDs... cops, when they stop somebody, they don't know what they got. Right?

Dan: "Can you get a Xeroxed copy of your driver's license?"

You can just get another one. If you have got a driver's license and you have lost it, you can go online, you can go to a library and go on a computer and send them the money and order a new one and get it, or just go down to the Highway Department and they can make you a new one right there. There is no need to have a Xerox copy because you can get it replaced for about 10 bucks or something. I'm not sure; they have a couple of different prices but it's less than 20 bucks, I know. But my point is everybody here should have a picture ID before they get out and you should ask your social worker when you are getting out, and that you need a picture ID if you do not have one.

Because the police, they don't know what they are dealing with; they don't know if you are somebody who is in trouble three states away if you don't have that ID. And they are justifiably frightened to be out there. I mean you think about what it would be like to be a cop or a highway patrolman at 10 o'clock at night. You pull somebody over on the interstate in the middle of nowhere. You don't know what is in that car. So you have to understand how they operate, the police; when you deal with them they are already operating at a high level of anxiety. And when people start showing out in front of them, it just makes their anxiety level go up. And people like me, who are kind of tall and kind of big have to be very, very careful and be very, very polite when I have those interactions with the police just so they do not think I am a threat. Because people who are big are seen as being threatening just because they are big. You can be the nicest guy in the world but if you are big, people tend to be frightened until they are shown differently.

What you do today you tend to do tomorrow. What you did yesterday you will tend to do today. So that is one of the reasons I talk about one of the behaviors you want to try to do is be on time to all the groups. Not because the groups themselves are so special or so important but because you need to be able to be on time when you get out, which gets back to the idea of being in the right place at the right time. And that when you are in the right place at the right time, you can't be in the wrong place at the wrong time. And I know this sounds really simple but you can take these ideas and build on them and say... I mean, how many people here have heard somebody say the phrase when they come back to the hospital, "Well, I was in the wrong place at the wrong time"?

Thomas: "I don't want to come back, man; I don't want to come back."

"I was in the wrong place at the wrong time." Well, who put you there? "Well, I did." Right? I mean everybody has a choice right? If

I stand up, I have a choice to walk this way or that way. Or to not walk at all. We all make decisions; every moment we are making a decision.

Thomas: "One thing about me, I go mentally ill, is I can't make all the decisions. I got to have somebody else to help make the decisions."

That's good; that's insight to be able to recognize that. The other thing that they talk about and is a big deal is the idea of having insight. Because having insight leads people to have good judgment. If you are mentally ill but don't have insight that you have a mental illness, I don't know what we can do... Julie, Julie... please sit up.

Julie: "I want to sleep."

No. You can sit up to play cards, so...

Julie: "I just sitting here listening and it's putting me asleep."

Well, you could interact.

Julie: "Interact with what?"

Make a comment. [Long pause.] Does any of this make any sense to you?

Julie: "Yes."

What parts?

Julie: "What you do today you tend to do tomorrow."

It's kind of like, doing what you are doing, that in itself is a behavior. If you tend to lay your head down in class today, you will tend to lay your head down in class tomorrow. So, do people react to that?

Curt J: "Yes."

People react to behaviors. If I do one thing, I get such and such reaction. If I do something else, I get another reaction. If you are able to be interested in playing cards and you have no problem doing that which is what you would be doing...

Julie: "Yeah, but I be doing things..."

Well, you can interact and get involved...

Julie: "I would like to get some water."

That will be fine. So all this stuff is, you know, they are nice words but if you don't practice them they don't do anybody any good. First you have got to understand it and then you have to put it into action.

Thomas: "Yeah."

(End of group)

So, to review:

Goal 1. Get Out.

Goal 2. Stay Out.

How?

Make your behavior match your goal.

And recognize that what you do today, you tend to do tomorrow. What you did yesterday, you tend to do today unless you make a change.

Also be in the right place at the right time, because all the times you are in the right place at the right time you cannot be in the wrong place at the wrong time.

3   *Dealing with Frustration*

So what, besides untreated mental illness, could keep us from keeping our behavior congruent or in line with our goals?

I believe the biggest danger is not learning to deal with frustration.

Frustration will lead to either…

Social confrontation or Social cooperation.

Where does frustration come from?

Usually from the belief that our needs are not being fairly met.

But I have some bad news.

The world isn't fair. If you have schizophrenia or bipolar disorder, that is not fair and you did nothing wrong. And the unfairness of having a mental illness by itself is frustrating, but you can have a good or even a great life. How good a life you have will depend on how you adapt or learn to take control of, as much as you can, your own situation. This manual's goal is to help you reach YOUR goals. And to reach your goals, you must first make a goal.

Frustration will lead to one of two behaviors: confrontation or cooperation.

Frustration

Social confrontation — social cooperation

The biggest cause of frustration is the feeling that you have been treated unfairly by someone and that someone "blows you off."

A simple exercise I have done with my patients is to have everyone stand up and each person announce, in turn, "I'm frustrated." Then the group turns their backs to that person. Each person takes a turn. When it was my turn, even though it was my exercise, I was amazed that I had a physical or body response; my face flushed!

Probably the worse frustrations will be at the hands of friends, family and your local mental health center, the exact people you would expect to be on your side. To give examples of each:

Friends: Some friends might not want to hang out with you anymore. Some might tease you. Some might be too careful around you.

Family: Families always have lots of buttons they can push and frustrations with dealing with families are best headed off by having good education available for your family about what your diagnosis is and how best to help you. The idea of families having lots of buttons they can push just means that close family members, because they are close family members, know better than anyone else our likes and dislikes, and what kind of talk will make us happy or sad or angry. Sadly, some families will see mental illness as a sign of being weak-minded or as a character flaw.

Mental Health Centers: Some staff will behave with a power-up attitude. This can be especially frustrating if you have more education than the staff person and that staff person treats you as being less than equal. I know of a patient who went to his appointment riding a bus 20 miles only to find out they had written down the wrong date for the appointment. He was supposed to be there the next day and they would not see him. They told him to come back the next day. What would you do in a situation like that? If you complain and the staff person blows you off, you will be even more frustrated. What then?

The key to dealing with interpersonal frustration is to BE HEARD. So what is interpersonal frustration? Simply the frustration that comes from people dealing with people.

So how does frustration lead to confrontation?

Isolation.
The person who isolates themselves from others does not have any way to BE HEARD. But everyone NEEDS to BE HEARD.

So the person who isolates himself with his frustration will UNLOAD on someone with the tiniest prick, like a balloon popping. We have all been in the situation of talking to someone and that person will get angry all out of balance with what we have said. And not only that, we have all done it.

Do not save up your frustration. Think of frustration as heat under a teapot. Teapots are designed to let off a little bit of steam at a time when they get hot. If the tea pot could not let off steam it would EXPLODE. Do not be an EXPLODING TEAPOT!

So here is the second key to staying out. When you are frustrated, BE HEARD. And real frustration happens when the person whom you think treated you unfairly refuses to hear you. So what then? Well, you can still be heard. Have friendships with others who are walking the same road as you. Listen to them express their frustrations and expect them to listen to you express yours. This is the way that frustration leads to social cooperation.

Goal 3: Build a Support Team

You must build a support team to be heard. You must have relationships where you will not be judged but will get honest feedback. Peer relationships are very important as are family and friends. Hopefully you will have members of your treatment team whom you feel you can be open with to help resolve feelings of frustration. But it does take effort and you cannot build a good support team if you isolate yourself. Take part in shopping trips or groups.

Smile.

One of the easiest ways you can positively affect your environment is to smile at other people. When you smile, you usually get paid back with a smile and just the fact of smiling makes you feel better.

Have a plan to deal with frustration before it comes and, believe me, you will have to deal with frustration. Frustration is something every person has to deal with—how well you deal with frustration will be a huge factor in how well you do.

There is an old expression, "Cutting off your nose to spite your face." What it means is that when someone is angry or frustrated and they act out on that frustration or anger, the person who tends to get hurt the most is the person acting out. If we react without letting off stream first, we mostly will just hurt ourselves. Have a way to let off steam when frustration comes and talk with someone on your support team to figure out the best thing to do. Don't just act out.

Group Discussion: Building a support team so frustration becomes social cooperation, not social confrontation.

You can build anything; like, as a kid, some kids build model cars, right? To build a model car, it takes an effort, you have to sit down and think how you are going to do it, what I am going to start with and how I'm going to proceed.

Building a support team is the same way. You have to think about it. It just doesn't happen; you have to put in some effort. Alright, someone builds a model car, what result are they expecting to get? Something to look at, to play with... Okay, if you are building a support team, what benefit are you expecting to get from the support team?

Different answers...

Help when I need it; I like that. So when you get help when you need it, who are you going to get help from?

Curt J: "From your neighborhood..."

John: "Everybody in my support team."

Thomas: "You get yourself to do it.

Alright, the best support team — is it going to be a one-way street or is it going to be a two-way street?

(Lots of answers)   "Two-way," "Two-way street."

So what does that mean?

Julie: "It's give-and-take."

Bingo, it's give-and-take. The strongest support teams are going to be…

Thomas: "A chair." [Everybody laughs]

No, it's not a chair… be nice… they are going to be interlocking, they are going to fit together.

Curt J: "You can't break it; it's like a chain or a puzzle…"

It will be interlocking, give-and-take. So who are you going to build give-and-take support teams with?

Larry: "Your family, your mental health center."

Keith: "Your doctor."

Cassie: "Your kids."

"Your pharmacist."

Lois: "Your sister and brother, your mother and father."

Keith: "Real friends, real friends."

Robert said it — someone you can trust.

Robert: "It's like you walk down a catwalk and watch pieces get pulled from your own body."

Cassie: "What are you talking about?"

He doesn't know; he loves the sound of his own voice and we tolerate it. [Everyone laughs] It's just wonderful to see someone… so in love. [Everyone laughs more.]

Someone you can trust, someone that can understand. Now, there is one person that no one has mentioned yet. You said, "mental health center?"

John: "I said 'higher power.'"

What did you say?

Keith: "Treatment team."

Who is going to understand...

Julie: "Spouse."

That's good; spouse.

Everyone names more "Social worker." "Doctor." ...

You are all missing one more...

"Nurse."

Come on, somebody...

"Santa Claus." [Everyone laughs.] "Preacher." "Yourself." "Your doctor." "The outreach clinic."

Each other. Who knows more about what you are going through other than you?

"Other peers."

Other peers. Who knows more about what you are going through than you?

And you go to a group home. Dan, you were just in a group home; how many people were there, peers?

Dan: "Sixteen."

How many staff were there?

Dan: "Probably about eight or nine. Not at one time."

How many at a time?

Dan: "About three."

About three. So it's 16 peers and three staff. Would the staff, if you had an issue, would they be willing to listen to you as much as a peer would?

Dan: "No."

No. Okay.

Jerry: "Yeah, but you got to be real careful about who you tell your business to."

I understand that; you do have to be picky. I'm not saying you tell everybody because not everybody can be trusted, not everybody is appropriate for one person. But, right, for each situation, some things you share with some people, some things you share with other people. And that goes back to the idea of interlocking support. If I just use Billy to tell all my troubles to, I'm going to overload him. 'Cause I got a lot of troubles. [Everybody laughs]

He's going to be, like, "Man, you wearing me out." Right? So I reach out to a lot of people. I reach out to the people that it is appropriate to reach out to with those issues. You try to build interlocking support with everyone so everyone can stand together, but the load is not too heavy on any one person.

There's 16 people in the group home. Now, this can be a well-functioning group of people or it can be a badly functioning group of people. So how do we make it a good functioning group of people?

Group answers "Communicate."

Communicate, that's good.

Thomas: "I got something. Like you was saying, we could get together and build a support system."

What I think is always good is if somebody can identify what their goal is… you know like we say what is our goal number one? "Get out." Goal number two is "Stay out." Well, when you get to a group home, I would think you would want to go in with the number one idea of getting everyone there to understand that the biggest thing we can do for ourselves is to be our own support team. Right?

[Discussion begins on givers/receivers and takers.]

Now, there are two basic kinds of people. There are a whole lot of people that can be called givers/receivers, right? Like, I talk to Billy a little bit, tell him some of my troubles; Billy talks to me a little bit and tells me some of his troubles. Okay? That makes me and him a giver/receiver to each other. But there are also people that are takers. And the biggest problem a group like our 16 people in the group home is going to have... any group that you have is going to be mostly givers/receivers, but inside any group of givers/ receivers, there are going to be a few people that are takers that are pretending to be givers/receivers. They are going to take advantage of the situation. So Billy comes and tells me all... let me see, how do I want to say this right?

I come to Billy and I tell him all my troubles. And then Billy comes to me and I'm, like, "Man, I ain't got time for that."

Julie: "That's a taker."

That's a taker. Right, that's a taker. And all of us have those moments when we feel like that, "I just don't want to be bothered right now," but what I'm talking about is that person who never gives back. And they will use the information to try to better their own situation. Or people like that will tend to promote chaos in the group because the more chaos that is produced, the easier it is to take. They will be the people that are putting people up against each other. Instigators. Who here has seen people that are instigators? That instigate trouble for the heck of it? Well, those people are takers because the idea of instigating trouble is: when you instigate trouble, there are more opportunities to take. The more chaos there is, the more opportunities there are to take advantage. When you go into a group situation or a group home, you want to build a support system. You want to make sure you are trying to build a support system with people that are givers/receivers. Now the terms "giver/receiver" and "takers" are just terms that I have made up and it doesn't really matter what we call it but everybody is familiar with the idea.

So when you are building a support system, you have to take care which peers you involve. Like Jerry was saying, you can't tell everybody your business. You can't tell your business to people that are going to use information that you tell to get you in trouble or promote their own agenda.

People pretty much know who they get along with, but people that are takers will often times disguise themselves. They will be very charming.

Like the guy might say, "Hey, man, give me 50 cents today and I'll give you 50 cents when we get paid." And you never see that 50 cents. And there is always a wonderful excuse why you never see it. And then they come again, "Oh, yeah, I remember, but if you give me 50 more cents today, I'll pay you back."

Harley: "It don't work two times around."

Yeah, that's what I'm saying, it really won't work twice but it will happen in more subtle ways.

So your goal, if we are talking about goals, goal number one is to "Get out" and goal number two is to "Stay out." Goal number three ought to be: Build that support system. Why? Because it's going to give you a place to go when you get frustrated. When I say, "Make your behavior match your goal," the biggest thing that is going to go against that is frustration. Being angry at somebody that you can't do anything about… it is about building that support system so you have a place to go. So one of the things you have to do is you have to be willing to talk to each other. Now that's a problem for some people because some people are very private. It's hard for some people to talk and we have to recognize there are those people like that. When we have those people around us, instead of trying to force them to talk, we should let it be known to them that we are willing to listen if they need us to listen. Those people that are really quiet and reserved and keep to themselves are not usually takers because they are not initiating stuff. The people that are takers are usually very talkative, charming and outgoing. Those are the people you usually have to worry about. With quiet people, the thing to do is offer to listen when they need someone to listen. Once they get relaxed enough to communicate, they will often be your most solid part of your support system. You just have to recognize that there are some people that tend to be, by nature, very quiet and reserved.

Letting that frustration lead to social cooperation means having built a support team to go to in time of need so the frustration does not lead to social confrontation.

Thomas: "There are people that hold their anger in. It's better to express yourself and let it out…"

Some people are like that.

Thomas: "Some times words bother one person but not the other…"

But words do hurt.

So I have to think about this if I want to make this my number three goal. But I think, "Getting out and staying out." But I think building that support team is just a different way of saying dealing with that frustration, letting that frustration lead to social cooperation and not social confrontation.

Judy: "Mr. Mann, if you are in a group of people that you don't really care about and no one can make you care about them, is that sad?"

Yeah…

Judy: "I said 'group of people,' I didn't say 'everybody.'"

Well, um… I understand what you are saying. I mean, lots of people get put in situations where they think, "I'd rather not be in this situation," but you have got to make the best of it. Make the best of the situation that you are in…

Judy: "Well, can you change it?"

Yeah, by being positive.

Judy: "And then you can move on."

Yeah, just try to be positive.

Judy: "In general."

Yeah. The idea is that, you know, the more positive you are, especially in one of these group things, the better everyone will get along. Because bad things will happen.

Thomas: "Good things and bad things."

That's just part of it. People are going to get on each other's nerves, but the more positive you are and if everybody is more positive, what does that do? That lifts everybody up. It lifts everybody up.

Harley: "Encouragement."

John: "And the sky is the limit."

Yeah, yeah…

Thomas: "It's the truth, you know. I don't know why you shouldn't tell the truth. You going to tell the truth anyway, you know… you know if you going to tell the truth, you might as well let it take you higher up."

Yeah.

John: "When I was at a residential care facility about 2… about 2-and-a-half years ago, uh, I had to report to Alcoholic Anonymous and… but the leader in Alcoholic Anonymous to my fortune, to my benefit before I came back here with my relapse, uh I used to be able to talk to him about anything. He'd say, 'Whatever you and I talk about, it remains between you and me.'"

Yeah.

John: "And he used to give me tips on little things that the average person, I mean, the average person wouldn't pay no attention to… things that lead to triggers and triggers lead to relapse."

Right.

John: "He tip me to small things that matter most."

Yeah.

John: "It isn't always big things, big things could be like a balloon; poke a hole in it and it will bust. Small things like a balloon that hasn't been blown up yet, it's not a big deal, so keep it like that, at that level. Don't let it turn into something big and out of control. Sometimes you need somebody to talk to, refer to concerning your diagnosis or your dual diagnosis using drugs or just plain old mental illness; you can always talk to your sponsor or someone, a member of your support team. Your father, your sister, your brother, niece, nephew, son, daughter. Somebody that you can really tell all the truth to and don't have to worry about repercussions."

That's true; that is what you are expecting from your support team.

Harley: "That's what makes it easy to tell someone about your situation is if you know there are not going to be any repercussions behind it."

Yeah, and that is what you want.

Thomas: "You have to understand, life is not going to change for you. You going to go through these problems because you have to, people going to try to comment on you, they tell good on you one day and then be bad the next day."

Harley: "Then again you don't want someone to lead you on thinking that when you tell them your problem or you tell them what's your situation afterward, they turn around and there are repercussions. I done seen people do that before you sit down and talk to them and think it will be alright, and then you turn around and… especially police officers and people like that. They tell you one thing but when the situation is over, at the end of the situation, it results in you are in trouble or things like that. It's like you said before, you got to know a person before you tell certain things to, some people you can't tell some things to."

Judy: "That's right."

Hartley: "You have to know who to talk to about what is bothering you."

Powerlessness versus empowerment. Kind of the idea that I am talking about is the feeling of being powerless. I know a lot of people here, probably most people here, feel powerless in this situation.

Thomas: "Right."

But what I'm talking about is, if you start to learn to count on each other as people that are going through the same thing that you are, you empower yourselves. You give power to each other to deal with these situations. As long as you remain in a situation where you feel that whatever happens to you, you have got to go to the treatment team or you have to go to the doctor. You have got to go to this, you have got to go to that to solve these problems, you always maintain yourself in this powerless situation. The place that you have the strongest power is from each other. If you can build a proper kind of peer support team when you go to a group home or assisted living, you will have a place to go for support without worrying about repercussions for saying the wrong thing.

It is important to be able to speak without fear about things you think about. Being able to speak openly with your peers allows you and your peers to understand that you are not alone. You have a shared experience and you can have shared solutions. These shared solutions will give you and your peers the power to help yourselves.

Harley: "Because they know the level that you are on…"

Right, right. They will understand better than anybody else.

Hartley: "Because some of them have been through the same thing that you have been through."

Yeah.

Thomas: "That's something like you know what they know but they don't want to… you know they don't want to say that they know what you know, you know, you got friends, other, you know, other cats out there knowing what they know, I meet somebody else that know somebody else, but altogether, still being late, you know…"

Let me ask you this. I got you. How many people here have seen somebody starting to relapse? Been around somebody starting to relapse? Everybody in here has seen somebody starting to relapse. Is it okay for you to do something… to go to the person and say or go to the treatment team and say so-and-so is starting to relapse. Who is going to see that happen first? You will. You will.

John: "Talk to that person."

Yes.

If you are in a group home and somebody starts to relapse, the staff isn't going to notice it first; they are not going to pick up on it first, you are going to see it. And you can help them, catch the problem when it's a little pebble in your shoe, not let it become a big rock. Right? When you are doing well, give the permission to those around you, "If you see me starting to slip, come to me and tell. Help me before I fall totally and have to go all the way back to the hospital." So you have to give permission and get permission.

Now, everybody here has probably seen somebody do that (relapse). Has anyone here ever done anything about it?

John: "It happened to me and I talked to some of my close peers, I talked to them about it."

That's a good thing; do something about it. When you see somebody starting to slip, don't wait until they have totally slipped. Catch them, catch them before they fall. You know. Do it for them, do it for yourselves. Catch each other before you fall.

Catch them before they fall. Catch each other before you fall. That is really what building a support team is about.

Harley: "A support team is to help you before any bad problems develop. That's what I think my support team is."

Good, good, alright, I guess we are done, thank you.

End of Group

In the previous group we talked about givers/receivers and takers.

How to avoid being exploited...

Exploited is a way of saying "being taken advantage of"... no one likes the feeling of being used by someone else just so the person using you can get something that you have that they want. So, how to avoid being used?

For our own protection, it is useful to see people as being divided into two different groups: givers/receivers and takers. Thankfully, most people are givers/receivers but there is a smaller group of people who pretend to be givers/receivers but are actually takers.

Givers/receivers give in-kind what they receive. Givers/receivers make good friends or acquaintances. If you loan them some money, you are sure to get it back. If you listen to them voice their frustration, they will listen to you when you need to vent your frustration. By being willing to both give and receive, givers/receivers make life easier, more relaxed and more fun. Givers/receivers are happy for you when you do well and you, if you are a giver/receiver, are happy for them when they do well.

So who are the takers? Takers pretend to be givers/receivers but never seem to be able to give back anything but excuses about why they can't really give back in-kind what they received. It's how they get through life — by taking advantage of those who are easy to exploit. Do not make the mistake of thinking you can change a taker into a giver/receiver. The only thing you can do, if you are taken advantage of, is to not let the taker take advantage of you again. Takers will lead you to greater frustration, not less. And unvented frustrations lead to behavior outbursts that can get you back into the system. So beware of the taker pretending to be a giver/receiver.

So, to review:

Goal 1. Get Out.

Goal 2. Stay Out.

How?

Make your behavior match your goal.

Frustration:

Have a plan to deal with frustration so that frustration will lead to Social Cooperation and not Social Confrontation.

Don't isolate yourself and do develop a support system that includes peer support.

Beware of Takers pretending to be Givers/Receivers.

4 *Be in the right place at the right time*

Many patients in psychiatric forensic hospitals have drug and alcohol problems that hurt their ability to manage their mental illness. Usually patients discharged from a forensic mental hospital will still have some type of legal hold over them by some type of court of law which requires continued treatment and random drug tests. Patients often "bounce back" because of failed drug tests. Others will use alcohol or other drugs that make them "high," and will re-offend and end up being sent back. Others will bounce back because something angered them at their placement group home and they act out in a way that gets them sent back. Most patients in forensic hospitals have burned their bridges with their families so they can't return home. Many patients who go to a regular mental hospital, however, usually go home to their families after the first onset of mental illness. Learning to manage your illness successfully at the beginning of your illness will keep bridges from being burned.

One way to keep from burning bridges is to be in the right place at the right time. The idea is a simple one. For all the times that you are in the right place at the right time, you cannot be in the wrong place at the wrong time. When I taught this in group, someone with a sense of humor would always say something to the effect of, "What if you are in the right place at the wrong time and, say, an airplane lands on you, or a meteor falls on your head or...?" Any of a number of unlikely things could happen but are very, very unlikely. So barring some really, really bad luck, all the times that you are in the right place at the right time, you cannot be in the wrong place at the wrong time. Unless a meteor lands on your head.

People who have problems with alcohol or drugs have a huge problem. They place themselves in the wrong place at the wrong time by putting themselves in dangerous situations where they will be tempted to use again. I remember a patient who had problems with crack cocaine and alcohol who went to a bar, not to drink, but because the bar was selling hot dogs, two for a dollar. So he went to the bar to eat hot dogs even though he had gone there in the past to drink and buy crack cocaine. He deceived himself by telling himself he would not drink or use drugs; he would just eat hot dogs. Professionals call this type of self-deceit (lying to yourself) as part of what is called "denial." People use denial to kid themselves or trick themselves into putting themselves in situations where they will be tempted to do what they know they should not do but really want to do. Like someone on a diet going to a candy factory "just to see" how candy is made.

He told himself he wouldn't use. After coming to the bar and eating the hot dogs, he was thirsty. Well, beer goes really well with hot dogs, so he thought to himself, even though he had told himself he wouldn't drink, just one would be okay. So he had one beer, then he had another and then ran into someone who had some crack who was an old friend… to make a long story short, this patient was back in the hospital about two weeks after he got out. The goods news is that he learned and realized how he played a trick on himself. And that is what people will do who abuse alcohol or other drugs. They will swear to themselves that they are strong and can handle temptation, and then they will deliberately place themselves in situations where they will be tempted to use.

But there is another danger. I had another patient who had paranoid schizophrenia and a history of crack cocaine abuse. She complained that the group home she was sent to was in the middle of a drug-infested neighborhood. She said she would walk outside and people were selling just down the street in plain view and she was constantly tempted. And she used and got sent back and, in her mind, she felt set-up by the placement chosen for her by the hospital staff. And I could not disagree with her. It is a fact that group homes tend to be in lower-income neighborhoods where there will often be street drugs.

Social workers are the ones who usually arrange for discharge placement. One of the problems social workers face is finding an open spot for someone to stay. Mental hospitals are under lots of pressure to treat and discharge patients as quickly as possible, even if it doesn't seem that way when you are in the hospital. But there are always untreated mentally ill persons in emergency rooms who need treatment in lockdown hospitals because they are felt to be dangerous to themselves or others. Because of the pressure of new patients who need treatment, social workers are usually forced to place patients ready for discharge in the first group home they can find. Of course, this is not a problem for patients who are going back to their families, but often there are many temptations in or near family homes. Plus, when patients are discharged back to their home neighborhoods, they already know where to go to get alcohol and other drugs, so sometimes, even if you can go home, it might be a better idea to go somewhere that you don't have street connections, to remove that temptation.

Be in the right place at the right time. Because all the times you are in the right place at the right time, you cannot be in the wrong place at the wrong time.

I had another patient who bounced back; he was mad at the group home staff where he was placed because they would not let him go to his uncle's funeral. This would make anyone angry. And the staff should have taken him to the funeral if at all possible, but this group home had a rule that you had to be there for a month before you could get passes to go places. And sometimes people use rules in too rigid a way and I think this group home was likely too rigid, but it is what it is.

Well, this patient had been there for almost the whole month and, on a planned trip to the store that the group home took the patients to every week so the patients could buy things such as snacks and cigarettes, he realized he was within a couple of miles of where a friend of his lived. She had been a patient at the hospital also, but had returned to live with her family. This patient, whom we will call Dan, walked out of the store, called a cab and went to her house just to talk because he was mad about not getting to go to his uncle's funeral. Anyway, she had been in the hospital almost a year before getting out and she knew what could make people bounce back and she told him while he was there, "You know they are going to send you back to the hospital, don't you?" And he was sent back to the hospital, which is how I learned the story. What is so bad is that as of the following weekend he would have been at the group home for a month, could have gone to see his friend with a pass and could have gone by himself. He allowed frustration — from not getting to go to his uncle's funeral — to give him an excuse to behave in a way that didn't match his goal of staying out of the hospital. His behavior didn't match his goal because he was frustrated and he let the frustration lead him to social confrontation by walking off from his group. And he placed himself in the wrong place at the wrong time and was sent back to the hospital.

Sadly, this kind of thing happens over and over. Patients will get frustrated or angry and do something that gets them sent back to the hospital. This is also a big problem for inmates in jails or prisons. They will be doing well, then something will happen that they think is unfair and they will act out in a way to show that they can't be treated like that and end up being sent back to jail or prison.

Group Discussion: Being in the right place at the right time.

Here's something we have not yet talked about, "coping strategies."

Have you heard this expression, "coping strategies"? Let's go around and find out, "What does this expression mean to you?"

Thomas: "Anger management."

Anger management. Okay.

Thomas: "How to deal with your relationships."

Barry: "How you deal with problems."

Curt J: "Take your medicine as prescribed."

Curtis: "Teaches you how to deal with something that might cause you not to be able to cope."

[Everybody laughs.]

Alright, let's look at this. We are talking about "mental illness" [writing on board)] — that's a funky-looking M. Mental illness. I guess we ought to kind of come up with a kind of a definition of what mental illness is… mental illness to me is really misreading the cues or signs in the environment. Okay, what is the environment? Well, the environment is everything that is going on around you. This is our environment that we are talking about right now. Right. We are in an environment. Alright? When people are locked up, what they call that, they have an actual term for people being locked up, where they have limited ability to come and go. They call that a structured environment. [Structured environments are also sometimes called closed environments.]

When you can control things for people who may not be able to operate well in an open environment, because there is too much

*stuff going on, [they] can often do better in a structured environ-
ment. So basically the theory, concept of this place, is that it is a
structured environment and here you learn coping strategies that
will let you operate successfully, hopefully down the road, in a more
open environment.*

Barry: "What if you always did deal with it effectively?"

You wouldn't be here.

Thomas: "Um, like simple things that you do could get you out of
trouble, you could escape that problem."

*Like one of the coping strategies that I am fond of is this idea of
being in the right place at the right time, okay? If you are in the
right place at the right time, all the times that you are in the right
place at the right time, you can't be in the wrong place at the wrong
time.*

Curtis: "How do you determine what is the right place?"

*Well, it's like today. Let's say you woke up today. And you think
mentally or you make a written list of "where am I supposed to be
today, what am I supposed to do?" Right? Say you got out, have
you ever missed a mental health appointment? Well, on those
days that you missed mental health appointments you were in the
wrong place at the wrong time. You were not in the right place at
the right time. When you miss those appointments, that sets you
up for failure. So being in the right place at the right time sets you
up for success if success is defined as being able to stay out. And it
really is how you define success. Because there are some people that
really like being in a hospital like this. They get institutionalized
and they are more comfortable in this kind of a setting.*

Elroy: "I ain't never seen nobody like that…"

Ralph: "There are plenty of them. Think about people that
have been in and out and bounce back, bounce back over and

over again, always a different excuse. Those people are usually institutionalized. They are more comfortable here and they will always find some way to sabotage themselves so they come back."

Right, what he said. On a lot of levels, it is a more comfortable place because all your decisions are made for you. It is scary being out there on your own, having to make all your own decisions; it's scary.

That's why there are so many people out there that have trouble with drugs and alcohol.

Barry: "Nobody ever has a problem with somebody drinking until somebody ain't got no money. If the person that is drinking ain't got no money or person that is not so happy with the person that is drinking ain't got no money."

Huh? Did that make any sense to you? [Looks at another client who raised his eyebrows at Barry's comment.] What does that mean? Do you know what he is talking about? Did you hear what he said? What did that mean?

Ricky: "They jealous because he's got money. And the next person jealous at…" [trails off]

Curt J: "They going to have to share the bottle. With liquor, there is usually a drinking partner."

Thomas: "Not getting in trouble, it is just that bad, um that they ain't got no money and the person that, how you going to deal with that, how you going to show those emotions, how you going to keep from robbing somebody or going home and going to sleep, you could be in the wrong place at the right time."

Alright, misreading… mental illness is misreading cues and signs from the environment so badly that you become, that other people see you as being a potential or possible danger to yourself or others.

Curt J: "Yeah, that is how it was diagnosed on me."

Well, that's the way it reads legally on a commitment paper. It's not like you ARE; it's just that we think you MIGHT be. You might be dangerous to yourself; you might be dangerous to somebody else. And the mental illness part is misreading the cues and the signs in the environment. Because what will happen… often times people will become paranoid and act on their paranoia. And their paranoia comes from things that they see in the environment that they are misreading; they are mis-seeing.

Curt J: "One thing that they said about me was that I was afraid of the dark. I went every night out of my apartment and walked to the convenience store just as fast as I could, speed walking. Get some exercise. Now, how am I afraid of the dark?"

[Class laughs.]

Are you even in this group?

[Everybody laughs. This patient often liked to sit in my groups, even if not assigned, for the entertainment values I think!]

Okay, so my other thing besides trying to be in the right place at the right time is this… check your reality. Check your reality with somebody else. Ask this person, "Did you see this like I saw it?" Like, I ask you what is bad about alcohol and you come up with "There is no problem with drinking as long as people got money."

Barry: "That ain't what I said."

That ain't what you said? That's what you said. Well, what does that mean? Tell me again what you said.

Barry: "What I said was, how come… I said, 'How come…'" [long pause]

How come…?

Barry: "How come nobody ain't got no problem with nobody drinking until somebody ain't got no money? Nobody ever says anything to the man… if any one of us in here had money, none of us would be in here. And we could drink to our heart's content and nobody would say anything to us if we had some money."

That is not true.

Barry: "It's basically true."

No, it is not. That is not true at all. I have worked in a drug and alcohol addiction setting, and, yes, you have people that have money that go there.

Barry: "I'm saying the majority."

No. What happens is if a person gets a serious problem with alcohol, friends or family of that person will intervene. They will intervene, they will go and say the person with the problem is a danger to themselves and that person needs some treatment.

Barry: "Drinking… you… alcohol is perfectly legal."

Thomas: "Now if I go out there and I got some money and I'm going out there and buy me some beer, I don't care if I take my medicine or not. Now that is something you have got to deal with so, what he is saying is, if you got money, it is legal to do it. You know what I am saying? That is what he is saying: once you got money, it is legal to do it, what were you trying to say?"

I understand what he is saying and, on one level, he is right. But on another level, he is not right.

Barry: "Yeah, I see that level too…"

Well, it's obvious if someone drinks and then they drive, they are breaking the law then.

Curt J: "And if they are taking their medicine, they are going to crash the car…"

Barry: "I haven't had a traffic ticket since 1979 and I am kind of proud of that, too…"

I thought you said you didn't drink?

Barry: "I don't drink, but I still see things."

You seem fixated on alcohol for someone that — you never ever drank?

Barry: "No, I was just saying that it is legal and you can do it and it is perfectly legal."

Did he answer my question?

Barry: "Yeah, I did. I said I don't drink."

No, what did I ask? I asked you, "Have you ever drank?"

Barry: "I ain't never drank anything to amount to anything; it don't amount to an alcoholic, it don't amount to a sociable drinker. It don't even amount to that."

How would you describe it?

Barry: "I don't drink."

If you are not drinking, what would you not be drinking?

Barry: "Grapefruit juice and orange juice. I drink that when I can get it."

What kind of alcohol would you not be drinking?

Barry: "What kind of alcohol would I be drinking if I was drinking?"

Yeah.

Gary: "Jack Daniels is what I'd be drinking."

[Cassie starts laughing.]

Barry: "But I don't drink nothing."

[Cassie laughs again.]

Barry: "Really, I don't. Let's see, the last time I drank was at the race in Darlington in 2007 and I drunk three Jack Daniels and that was all I drank in probably three years."

Okay, so back to what I was talking about, coping strategies. One of the easiest things that will help Curt, for instance, and everybody in here, is being in the right place at the right time. And like what Curt said, "What does that mean, being in the right place at the right time?"

That means being where you are expected to be and be there on time. These groups, as I have gone over with everybody here or most everybody here that have heard my little talk about attendance, the groups themselves are not as important as actually coming to the groups and being on time, because it gives you the practice of being in the right place at the right time.

Curt J: "Like work?"

Yes, like work.

Barry: "I've worked since I was 16."

Barry, you always, you never say anything else, though. There is more there, there is more history than the little snippets that you offer.

Barry: "What? I really don't."

When somebody says, "I have" lived however long you have lived and then they tell you about this little part of their life and they say that is all there is, people start to wonder about, "What about all this other part?"

Barry: "I been at work all the time, 28 years."

That's what you always say.

Barry: "That's what I always do."

And nobody has got a clue why you are here.

Barry: "I don't have a clue."

[Cassie and class laughing.]

Truer words have never been spoken. [Everybody laughs.]

Barry: "I never missed a day of work before. I never been late. I don't know how this happened to me."

Check your reality. What I mean by that is talk with other people to see if they see things the same way that you do... and part of it is people, when they become ill, they tend to close off because it's scary and they don't want to share things; they don't want to be recommitted. They don't want to come back, so they get even more closed off and thinking their own thoughts and standing over [moves away to corner of the room away from everyone else] but if you can check your reality by talking with other people and seeing how other people talk about it, you can get a better idea of the proper signs and cues in the environment. So by checking your reality with other people... check your reality with others [writes this on the board] you can get a clearer understanding of the cues and signs in the environment. Just make sure that you are seeing it correctly. If you are having ideas that... I don't know... how many people here know that they have had some kind of delusions that were not real?

Greg: "I drunk some water out of a ditch one time and saw some spirit people. I started running down the road."

Curtis: "You drank some water out of a ditch?"

What possessed you to drink water out of the ditch?

Greg: "I was hunting one day and it was hot and I didn't carry no water with me and that water was running out of the ditch. It was running right; I crept down there and the next thing you know I was having delusions. I started running. I was scared of people then."

You were paranoid. And that's what I am talking about; they were not really after you, you were paranoid and if you had been able to check your reality before you got so scared that you started running from people you might not have had that problem.

Greg: "I tell something else that will give you that too, old lettuce…"

Did you say "lettuce"?

Greg: "That what a nurse told me: you eat that lettuce and it is old, you can have delusions on that too."

Curt J: "I had a delusion one time that my family was after me when I was on the outside of the house and I was running down the road from them and finally they caught me. And I ended up in the hospital."

'Cause you were scared.

Curt J: "I was scared to death of them; they were trying to make me take pills."

Well, there is one right there. A lot of people that are mental patients will be afraid to take their medicine because they think people are trying to what? Poison them…?

Curtis: "Yep, I've seen that. They think it is a government experiment."

Curt J: "I've…" [talking over Curtis.]

Let other people talk. Tell them what you said. Let everybody hear it.

Curtis: "Secret government experiment…"

How many people here have heard that? I have heard that a bunch of times. That the government has got us here to [whispers] to experiment on us.

Curt J: "By a mad doctor."

[Class leader makes B-movie mad doctor laugh.]

Curtis: "You are a scientist here under the guise of a teacher to observe us."

Riiiight.

Curt J: "You got a little camera on us sitting somewhere."

Well, people believe that and that is one of the hard parts of treating people that are mentally ill. It is that they will have paranoid beliefs and think that their food is poisoned. I mean, that is one of the first things they will think: that someone is poisoning their food or someone is coming in their house when they are not there. You know they forget that they moved something from here to there and they come back and find it over here instead of over there, and they say [whispers], "Huh! Somebody has been in the house!" And they start looking and they just start getting these feelings of dread and then they start acting on these feelings of dread and get into trouble and people perceive them to be a possible danger to themselves or others. So that is what I mean by checking your reality with other people.

I guess another way to say it, an easy way to say it is, talk it out. Try to talk it out with people. Talk about your fears. Talk about what you see in the environment and see if other people see the same things in the environment. You know it is like if people were scared on 9/11 that people were flying planes into buildings, well, yeah. There is a time to be paranoid.

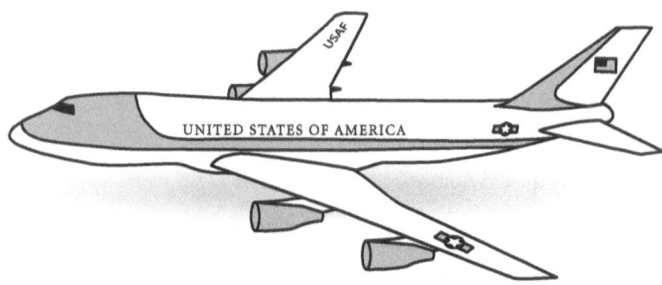

When they flew that plane up in New York and people didn't know it was Air Force One and everybody started running for their lives, panicking because they didn't know. They misjudged the environment; they didn't know that was Air Force One because no one had told them. They thought there were more terrorists trying to fly into a building. So it scared people. If people had talked about it, people would not have been scared; they'd go, "Oh, there's the President's plane." So they made a mistake in not sharing that information.

Alright that will do it, thank you.

End of Group

To review:

Goal 1. Get Out.

Goal 2. Stay Out.

How?

Make your behavior match your goal.

Frustration:

Have a plan to deal with frustration so that frustration will lead to Social Cooperation and not Social Confrontation.

Don't isolate yourself and do develop a support system that includes peer support.

Beware of Takers pretending to be Givers/Receivers.

Be in the Right Place at the Right Time.

PART TWO

In Part Two, we will talk about what mental illness is, denial, acceptance and how to take care of yourself with some simple nutritional advice. We will also talk about three over-the-counter supplements that are effective if taken correctly and are always safe.

We will also briefly list typical professional treatment team members and their roles.

5   *Mental Illness, what is it?*

Mental illness, as far as we know, has always been with us. Mental illness, however, is not seen for what it is but rather the stereotypes that have been passed down through the centuries.

It has long been known that a person thought "possessed by spirits" could drink healing water and become well, hence the belief in all cultures of "healing waters." It may have helped that some of these waters had lithium salts.

Some still believe that mental illness is spirit possession or, worse, is due to poor character.

So what is mental illness?
Mental health professionals use ideas called medical models and behavioral models to talk about mental illness.

The medical models deal with how chemicals in the brain, called "neurotransmitters," work. The "neuro" in this word refers to individual brain cells called "neurons." The transmitter part refers to how these individual brain cells talk to or signal each other. There are small gaps between the neurons and the neurons release chemicals into these gaps to signal to other neurons. These gaps are called synapses. These chemicals are what we call neurotransmitters. Mental illness is often spoken of as being a chemical imbalance. The term "chemical imbalance" suggests that the neurons release the wrong amounts of neurotransmitters or the neurons have problems with reading the chemical signals correctly. Different imbalances cause the symptoms we see in schizophrenia, bipolar disorders, depression and, really, whatever mental outlook anyone has is dependent on the balance of their neurotransmitters.

So mental illness to me is when someone's neurotransmitters are so out of balance that a person is unable to function well in their day-to-day living. Recovery, therefore, would be a return to functioning well in their day-to-day living.

Persons committed to mental hospitals are thought to be functioning so poorly in their day-to-day living that others worry that the mentally ill person may be dangerous to themselves or others.

The goal of giving medicines to mentally ill persons is to help rebalance their neurotransmitters so the mentally ill person can function better in their day-to-day living.

So what about behavioral models? There is a saying I like:
"Form follows function and function follows form."

Just like neurotransmitters and how they are balanced affects how someone behaves, how someone behaves affects their neurotransmitters.

How someone behaves affects their neurotransmitters.
For example, the behavior of smiling causes a typical pattern of neuron signaling or release of neurotransmitters. Frowning causes a different type of release. What this means is a person's behavior also affects their neurotransmitters.

Form follows function and function follows form. This is kind of the point of this entire book and the idea that form follows function and function follows form is how I started thinking about:

Make your behavior match your goal.
When you make your behavior match your goal, not only are you going to get closer to your goal — you are also going to gain some control of your neurotransmitters! And if you combine that control with the rebalancing of some well-chosen medicines, you can do quite well indeed!

So how does a person who finds themselves afflicted with mental illness and in an acute hospital get out and avoid the stigma of having been in the hospital?

The answer is easy but the practice is hard. The mentally ill person who does not want to be stigmatized must alter their behavior as much as possible to fit into society. The more easily and completely you can fit into society, the less stigma you will suffer.

Some will say this is unfair, that society should be changed through education to accept the mentally ill as mentally ill and make allowances for behavior that strays from the norm. This solution is not only not possible, it is also unwise. Why?

Because the more someone strives to behave "normally," the more "normal" they will become. It has long been known, but not widely acknowledged, that brain chemistry follows behavior. The more "normal" someone acts, the more "normal" they will become.

So what is "normal"?
There is actually a wide range of what would be considered "normal." Otherwise we would have to pick one person as the model for "normal" and everyone else would be abnormal.

Also there is the idea of what is "normal" for you? Think about a person who is good at math but suddenly could not do math. That would be abnormal for them. But many people find doing math challenging, so that would be normal for them.

So we must remember that behavior rules are actually quite broad. Plenty of people have odd thoughts or strange beliefs. Someone who does not believe in God will think those who do are deluded or delusional but both beliefs are acceptable to have in today's society. So an atheist believes Christians, Muslims and Jews are all delusional, but these delusions are acceptable to have as the

Christians, Muslims and Jews will think atheists are delusional, but acceptable to have in society. Therefore delusional thinking of some nature (whether God exists or not) is already accepted in society. Clearly, delusional thinking is not the problem. The problems are caused by acts based on delusional thinking. Atheists may be thought delusional by believers but atheists have never blown religious people up with bombs because the religious people believed differently than the atheists. The same cannot be said of Christians, Muslims or Jews. The delusion is not the problem; it is the negative acts based on the delusion.

So can positive acts be based on delusions? Atheists would insist belief in God is delusional, but they could not deny millions of persons have been clothed, fed and educated through charity by Christians, Muslims and Jews.

It is how a person acts or behaves that gets them in trouble. Anyone can believe or think anything they want — it's the act, not the thought, that gets them in trouble.

So how do we stay out of trouble? There is an old saying:
"When in Rome do as the Romans do."

Well, what does this mean? It's very simple really: try to behave like the others around you to fit in. And by others around you, I mean others in society. If you go to the store but get tired should you just lie down? Of course not. The more your behavior is different from those around you, the more likely the others will want to separate you from themselves.

Delusions:

Where do delusions come from?

Delusions are like a house of cards built on one faulty idea. The faulty idea comes from a belief based on something actually seen or heard. As an example, let's look at kids in the eighth grade. Kids that age are going through many changes and these changes make them very focused on themselves, which is totally understandable. Their bodies are changing, their minds are changing, their interests are changing — almost, it seems, on a daily basis. Peer relationships and what others think of them become very important. It is totally common for eighth-grade kids to go to the cafeteria, for example, and overhear conversations and think the conversations are about them. Eighth-grade kids are "egocentric." Ego means "self" and centric means "center," but "egocentric" is different from "self-centered." Self-centered people only care about themselves, not about others. Egocentric people are worried about how others see them. Also egocentric persons think of themselves as "different" from other people, although we know the eighth graders all feel "different" in the same way!

Voices and delusions:

But the person who suddenly starts hearing voices will feel themselves to be different also and may believe they hear spirits or ghosts or God. And once a person starts hearing voices, that person may develop the belief that they have information, important information, only they have access to and therefore the information should be guarded and hidden so that no one else will steal it or use it. And as they guard this information, their thinking becomes based on this special knowledge known only to them. And this idea is the faulty card upon which the deck of cards is built.

So where do voices come from?

I have thought and thought about how to easily explain where voices come from but failed until I thought about it from a musical perspective or viewpoint. I have played guitar for years and recorded music and mixed music for rock bands. The problems with putting microphones on drum kits is that each microphone will "hear" not only the drum it is pointed at but also all the other drums.

This ends up making a "mish mash" of noise because if you use several microphones, each on a different drum, not only do you hear the drum each microphone is aimed at, you will hear as background all the other drums through each microphone. All those background drum sounds make it hard to get a good, understandable drum kit mix. To solve this problem, a device called a "noisegate" was invented. Each microphone is aimed at a sound source, then runs into a noisegate. The noisegate turns off the microphone until the drum the microphone is aimed at is hit. When a microphone's drum is hit, the noisegate opens and lets that sound through, then closes again to block unwanted sound. The noisegate only allows a certain volume to go through and anything below that level is turned off and ignored.

Human beings have a biological noise gating system called the P50 auditory gating system. Like the mechanical noisegates I would use to block unwanted drum noise, a person's P50 auditory gating system blocks much of the background noise in the environment from the perception of the person. The P50 auditory gating system allows us to pay attention to a conversation in a noisy environment like a noisy restaurant or to not pay attention to all birds singing in a park on a spring day unless we want to pay attention.

So what does this have to do with hearing voices? The P50 auditory gating system does not work properly in persons who have schizophrenia. This means the schizophrenic person is unable to suppress background noise like other people. The schizophrenic person's brain tries to deal with that excess noise and ends up interpreting that noise as voices.

Almost everyone has had the experience of thinking they heard someone call their name, especially when they are tired. This common experience is an instance of the person's P50 auditory gating system letting through some sound that would normally be filtered from our attention. When that stimuli gets through, our brain tries to interpret that sound into something meaningful to us and so we think we hear someone call our name. The schizophrenic person is constantly subjected to an overload of stimulation that should be filtered from his or her attention. Their brains interpret this overload into hearing voices.

Smoking and voices and P50 auditory gating
Persons with schizophrenia often smoke and have lots of trouble trying to quit. Nicotine temporarily corrects the problems that persons with schizophrenia have with P50 auditory gating. Persons who hear voices and have delusions will have less problems with voices and delusions when they are smoking. This benefit from smoking makes it even harder for the person with a mental illness such as schizophrenia to quit smoking. I have looked everywhere I can think of to find something that will correct the P50 auditory gating deficit. The only thing besides nicotine that I know of that

will correct P50 auditory gating, however, is clozapine which has its own issues. One possible option would be the new electronic cigarettes that are now available that deliver nicotine in water vapor so those e-cigarettes would allow the person who could not quit smoking to at least avoid the harmful tar in real cigarettes.

Complex thinking:

As the house of cards is built, the thinking will become more and more complex. The person may try to share some of their new knowledge with others, but will not like the response they get so they will begin to isolate themselves and their thinking will continue to get more and more complex. Finally, if the person acts upon this thinking they will likely find themselves in a psychiatric hospital of some kind. Or in jail.

Delusions without voices:
What about the person who has delusions but never heard voices? This is not uncommon. What is common between the two groups, however, is a misbelief about some part of the external or outside environment. Based on that misconception, a reality belief error is formed.

What is a reality belief error?
Simply, it is a belief that something is real that is not real. For example, a person may believe beings from other planets are talking to them through some hidden way known only to them.

Some persons will cling harder to beliefs if the beliefs have cost them their health or their families or their jobs. In other words, because they have lost things most important to them, because of their reality belief error or delusion, they will cling to the delusion as a form of compensation for their other losses. So persons with reality belief errors should not be allowed to hold those beliefs as harmless because they are not. Peers should also help challenge those beliefs.

When a person has become so divergent in their thinking that other people have serious concerns that the person with divergent thinking may be dangerous to themselves or others, the person with divergent thinking may be committed in a treatment center for evaluation. Once committed, a person will go before a group of people called the treatment team. The people on the treatment team will speak with the committed person one-on-one and also in a group setting where the committed person's care plan will be developed. The care plan will attempt to outline the treatments the treatment team thinks will return the mentally ill person to a level of functioning that will allow the mentally ill person to be treated in the community.

The Treatment Team

The people assigned the task of helping the seriously mentally ill person recover are the treatment team.

Who is on the treatment team?

The Prescriber. The prescriber will be either a doctor or a nurse practitioner or a physician's assistant. They will choose which medicines you should take and to which clinics you should go.

The Nurses. The nurses will make sure you receive the correct medicines and that you go to the correct appointments. They will also teach you about your medicines.

The Social Workers: The SWs will be your contact with courts if you are an emergency admission. They would also help you get a financial package if you need one for any group homes or other living situations if you can't go home to your family. Persons judged disabled by their mental illness can also get funding. When you are ready to get out of the hospital, your social worker will set up your follow-up appointment at your local mental health center.

The Psychologist: The psychologist may have you take certain paper and pencil tests to help the treatment team learn how best to help you.

What is your role on the treatment team?
Be as honest in your answers as possible. Write down questions you have for the treatment team before you go. Everyone forgets when they go to the doctor to ask all of the questions they wanted to ask unless they write down the questions and take those questions with them. Don't be afraid to ask questions; it will show that you are interested in your own treatment.

Learn the names, dosages, effects and side effects of the medicines you are taking. Write down the names and the dosages and the diagnosis for each medicine.

As you try different medicines, keep track of the medicines that seem to "agree" with you the best. Remember which ones you didn't like. Remember and share if you have ever had an allergic reaction to any medication. Remember and share if any medicine has caused you side effects that would make you want to stop taking that medicine. You should talk about any side effects you think you are having that may be caused by the medicines you are taking even if you don't think that the medicines are causing the effect that worries you. Side effects could include:

Feeling stiff; feeling sleepy or drowsy. Feeling hungry all the time; having heartburn or feeling as though you need to throw up. Having constipation or having problems with urination, dry mouth or drooling. Sexual problems are side effects. For men, these problems could include not being able to get an erection or keep an erection. For men and women, side effects could include less interest in sex or not being able to achieve orgasm. In fact, the main reason anyone stops taking any medication is because of sexual side effects. So if you are having these problems, you should tell your provider.

How to approach your treatment team.

Treatment teams can be scary. The people at that table are making decisions about your life, such as what medicine you will be taking, when you will get out, where you will live.

Don't be afraid to share. The more you open up, the more you speak freely and honestly about what is going on with you, the sooner the treatment team will develop confidence in you as a person. That probably seems strange — why should you as a patient care if the treatment team has "confidence" in you? The answer is simple: the sooner the treatment team feels it can trust you to follow through with your treatment, the sooner they will be comfortable with you being discharged from the hospital.

6   Denial and acceptance

The biggest barrier to recovery when someone first gets sick is denial. In the previous group discussion, Barry denies he has a problem with alcohol, but always talks about how he doesn't drink or have a problem with alcohol. This is why Cassie laughs when Barry is asked what he would drink if he were drinking and he answers "Jack Daniels." Barry denies he has any problems but is in a psychiatric hospital for criminal behavior. Before he can begin his recovery, he has to accept that he needs treatment. Barry has what is called a "dual diagnosis." He has mental illness and he has a substance abuse problem. At this point in his treatment, he was denying he had either problem.

Denial of illness is a normal thing for people to do. And not just for persons who have mental illness or substance abuse problems.

People who are newly diagnosed with cancer often have problems at first accepting their illness. Many persons with high blood pressure will deny that they have the problem and will not take medicine to control their blood pressure and will then have heart attacks or strokes that could have been avoided.

No one wants to believe they have a serious illness or problem. It hurts our feelings and how we see ourselves. But before we can have a successful recovery or successfully manage a chronic illness we must accept we have the problem. Acceptance also means allowing others to help you.

Group Discussion: Denial and acceptance.

Understanding your treatment… this is actually pretty easy…

John: "It would have to coincide with you knowing that are you mentally ill in the first place."

That's a good point. So understanding your treatment would have to start with the pre-requisite that you understand that you needed treatment.

John: "Yeah."

I like that. You have to understand that you need treatment.

Alright, if we first start off with the idea that first, to understand your treatment you have to understand that you need treatment, that makes sense, that's a good idea. Does anybody here not already understand that? Everybody is good with the idea that yes, I have a mental illness and yes, I need treatment for the mental illness?

Demarcus: "I was going to say that first you got to come out of the denial."

Yes, you have to come out of the denial.

Demarcus: "And acknowledge that you do have a disease and..."

That you need treatment, I just abbreviated treatment, trt. [Patient is reading board.]

Larry: "You need to understand that part of your treatment is to take your medicine."

Thomas: "What can you do to understand more about your treatment?"

Understand, I wrote fast and left out a couple of letters, sorry.

John: "You wouldn't give, you wouldn't give Haldol as a treatment to someone with heart disease."

No, you would weigh the benefit versus risk. But let me, let's jump, let me jump because I want to throw this at you. Alright. First you have got to understand that you need treatment. Once you get there, what you have got to understand is, "What is the goal of my treatment?"

Curt J.: "To get better."

Ah, that's too easy. What is the goal of my treatment?

Jeff: "To recover."

To recover. I like that.

Demarcus: "What I don't understand is, when they say 'to recover' what does that mean?"

Exactly, what does that mean?

Demarcus: "Yeah, does it mean to stay better for a minute, temporarily or to recover like you broke a arm or something like that...?"

That… I get that, what he just said really kind of cuts to what I think about it, too. What does "recover" mean? I mean, someone breaks his arm, he recovers from having a broken arm and his arm is no longer broken. Right? The problem with mental illness is right now there are no cures.

Curtis: "You stay in recovery for a lifetime, maintaining your level of recovery."

Right. You have to recognize that mental illness is a chronic condition. It's a chronic condition. It means it is ongoing. You have to manage it over time. It doesn't go away. Like a broken arm, you break your arm and it is a short-time illness, right? If you have mental illness like schizophrenia or bipolar, it's a chronic illness… and lots of people have chronic illnesses. If you have got high blood pressure… well, if you have high blood pressure, you have a chronic condition. Because you don't get high blood pressure and go, "Well, I got it for a couple of weeks and it is going to get better and go away." People, once they develop high blood pressure, they have to keep taking medicine to control their blood pressure. Right?

Demarcus: "How do you catch high blood pressure? Is it from eating too much sweets or something like that?"

Um, a lot of it is genetics. A lot of it is just, you know, your ancestors. A lot of it has to do with diet. But, just like any other kind of disease process, some people are set up genetically to have that kind of a disease. Chronic illnesses… let's look at this… chronic illnesses are managed… well, what does that mean? Well, that means you have to have a plan. They talk about the treatment plan and all these things; well, we have to have a plan of how we are going to take care of it, your acute episodes, and episodes or periods where you are in recovery and you are doing things.

But what I want to talk about is what is the goal? To me, the goal is figuring out, well for ME, what is MY best case outcome?

Curtis: "That is going to depend on the person."

Right, right.

Curtis: "What you are saying is it is going to be different for each person."

Right.

Curtis: "Some people are not going to need as much maintenance as some persons to be... functional, functional."

Did you hear what he said? That it is different for each person and that some people need more management and some people need less management. Some people will need more help at some times, less at others. So the goal of my treatment is going to be personal. It is going to be "What is the best case for me?" I mean, what is the best case for my situation for me to get to... where is it that I want to be?

Larry: "For me it is to conform my behavior to where I can stay out in the community."

That's good. What Leroy said is "to conform my behavior" where he can stay out in the community. That's a wonderful goal, right? And once you get to that point, you can decide, "Well, what am I going to do with my time?" But what he just said, "I want to be able to conform..."

Curt J.: "Conform to what?"

Well, really to conform to community standards. What does conform to community standards mean?

Curtis: "Not violating the rights of others. Not acting out. Not being homicidal."

Yeah, not being homicidal is a big one. [Everybody laughs.] It upsets people when you go out and kill people.

Curtis: "Not breaking the general laws of the land."

Or being suicidal.

Raymond: "Not harming yourself or others."

That's good ,that's in the commitment papers, danger to himself or others. Danger to herself or others.

Curtis: "As long as you don't break the civil or county laws which are actually federal laws you be alright, you know?"

Yeah.

Thomas: "Like you say, don't be harmful to yourself…"

Hello Benard, you want to come in?

Benard: "Can I go over there where the party is at?"

It's not a party. They are having "music and relaxation."

So… I like all of those. Understand that you need treatment, number 1. Then figuring out what is the goal of my treatment. And really the goal is going to be the best case for me, but within whatever the best case for me is, you have to conform to community standards. Which really means managing your behavior, which gets back to what I have talked about before. Why do you take medicines? What is the whole point of taking medicines? The whole point of taking medicines is that they help you manage your behavior so you can conform to community standards, so you can think clearly enough to make proper decisions, so your behavior does not get you in trouble. It's like I said before, there is no law against hearing voices. It is not illegal to have delusions. It can be uncomfortable, it can be upsetting to the person that is hearing voices or that has delusions. But as long as you are not acting upon the delusions in a negative way toward society, nobody should be able to say anything about it. The problem is that people that are mentally ill start to act on those beliefs, start to act on hearing voices, and it is almost inevitable that something is going to happen. What happens is people get placed under stress and they get upset and they act in a way that gets them in trouble. Go ahead, I'm sorry...

Demarcus: "Well, what I about to say, um, like when, um..."

I'm sorry, that's my fault. I should have let you talk when you raised your hand.

Demarcus: "Like when people get mentally ill, I said, it's like is it just for a short-term period? I'm saying like from a short-term period to like..." [says to self] "com'n man... man, go ahead..."

No, go ahead... well, let me try to answer what I think... people, when they get mentally ill, they will have, like, an acute episode. Where they are really having bad psychotic thoughts and all that means is that they are having thoughts that don't match up with the reality of the environment that they are in. You know it's like, "Well, I believe the FBI is after me and I got a wire in my brain..."

Demarcus: "I got it."

Okay, go ahead.

Demarcus: "Like somebody gets, become, um, goes to the, um, mental health department because they are paranoid and the doctor diagnoses him as paranoid schizophrenic. Okay, to look into the reason why they are paranoid instead of saying, 'Well, do you hear voices or do you such and such...,' could it be that somebody could be after this person?"

[Room starts laughing...]

No, no... I got you. There is an old joke: "Just because you are paranoid doesn't mean that there isn't somebody out to get you."

Demarcus: "Yeah, I've heard that before."

Yeah, it's an old, old joke. And it's true. I mean sometimes people are out to get you. But when people start…

[A couple of patients start singing a song, "Rumors…"]

Curt J.: "You would have to know the song."

What is the song? There are a bunch of different songs named "Rumors," probably not the one I'm thinking of.

Demarcus: "What I'm saying is you know people be out there, most of us have been on the corner, you know what I'm saying, drinking forties [40-ounce cans of beer], smoking blunts or popping pills or…"

I know what you are talking about. There is paranoia that comes from living in that environment naturally because people are trying to beat each other out of stuff and people are trying to take advantage of other people and, if you have a tendency to be paranoid anyway, it just fuels the paranoia that you already naturally have…

Curtis: "You are justified being paranoid given the environment."

Demarcus: "Like, if the police, I'm saying y'all doing your thing on the corner and so the police will try to charge you with trespassing."

Yeah. People that are participating in criminal behavior or behavior that could be called criminal by the authorities are going to feel paranoid about that behavior being found out…

Demarcus: "Yeah…"

I mean, people that drug users and people that steal, they always are dealing with some level of paranoia because they do not want to get caught, right? They have a natural paranoia. That is different from the paranoia that someone has paranoid schizophrenia. Now, a person who is paranoid schizophrenic who is in that situation

*is likely to react even worse than someone else would, okay? They
would just kind to tend of go way off the deep end, real easy...
someone that has paranoid schizophrenia, they have an idea that
they start with that they start building systems around and all
these beliefs that these people are "out to get me" and these people
are "out to get me" and those people over there "are talking about
me," when these people don't know anything about you, you know?
It's like, when you were in high school, when people were in high
school or junior high school or middle school, remember in junior
high and everyone was worried about "How's my hair?" and
"What do I look like?" and "Does so-and-so like me and so-and-so
don't like me?" and you would go in the cafeteria and a bunch of
kids over there, talking, and you are sitting down with your tray
and right as you sit down with your tray, they start laughing and
you are like, "Are they laughing at me?" Anybody ever had that
feeling when they were a kid?*

[Patients around the room agree that happened to them as kids.]

*Well, that's paranoia. And that is something that adolescents have
when they are in that stage of life, that's natural for them to feel
because they are at the age where they have the hormones going
on, they don't know how to judge reality anymore from being
a little kid and turning into a man or a woman, so it is a really
strange place to be. Well, that is kind of like when someone has
paranoid schizophrenia — they have that, only it's multiplied.
That feeling, those environmental clues like someone laughing,
everything that goes on in the environment is interpreted as having
some relationship to you. It's like, "Oh, that means something,
that bird flying over there means something!" and all these things
you start believing and it starts wrapping around, wrapping
around, wrapping around, and you start working on it. You get
this interpretation of what is going on around you going on in your
own mind and it gets bigger and bigger and bigger, and growing
until you feel forced to act. "I have got to act. I have got to do*

something. I'm scared." Right? And then you act out and then your behavior... and people are like, "WHOA, what's that about?" And they start talking to you and you start talking about, "And this happened and this happened and then the bird and then..." and they are like, "Okay, this guy or girl has paranoid schizophrenia, they need treatment." And then so you come and you get treatment and you start to go... and the toughest thing is people that do have paranoid schizophrenia, usually takes them a long time to get out of denial compared to other people because they have invested so much time building up that system, they kind of have to discard this idea and discard that idea, and come to the point where they can accept, "Oh, it really isn't all about me, it didn't mean that. I misinterpreted that."

Demarcus: "Let's say, let's say you was talking you being clowned on all the time, say like you live in the city and on your block everybody got nice clothes, whatever, you know, but, um, you don't have what they have so you go to school, you don't have what they have and then they poke fun at you and stuff like that, but it really don't bother you, then it just makes you feel bad so, um... I'm, you know, what I'm saying, paranoid to me is like in my situation is when I was young I used to steal out of stores and stuff like that like a criminal, criminal behavior..."

Umhum, yeah, there is a paranoia that goes along with criminal behavior that's not the same as the paranoia that goes along with paranoid schizophrenia. But they can overlap, I mean if you have paranoid schizophrenia and you are also doing criminal behavior, you are going to have paranoia from both areas.

Demarcus: "And see, then you going to add on top, on top of things, what I'm saying, to me to go through treatment, but I feel like if the doctor would sit down and talk to me, you know what I am saying, um, to get the right information and diagnose me, if you can have a diagnosis, if you speak to me you know what

I am saying, about my childhood, you, what I'm saying, I was diagnosed, you know what I am saying, and how I feel now like I first told them when they tried to put me on medication the first time, you know, I was, like, you know, I am from a rough neighborhood, you know what I am saying, if I am slow, you know what I'm saying, I can end up getting hurt. I don't need no medication that is going to slow me down because I need to be on my Ps and Qs at all times but they didn't want to listen, you know, they put me on the medicine like I was the head leader of my little neighborhood gang and stuff like that, I would be the one to tell them to do this or do that, you understand what I am saying, you know, keep dealing with the money, stuff like that. When I came home on that medication they were like, "Ah man, what happened to you? You don't need to take that stuff, man, you changed. You don't need to take that stuff if you could only see how you look man, you don't look right, you don't sound the same." I stopped taking it and my parents would be like, "Are you taking your medicine? Well, did you take your medicine, did you take your medicine, I see you ain't acting right." You know what I'm saying, I think it was just something, you know what I'm saying because they were scared of me, my parents were scared of me for what I was doing on the street so what they did, they tried to find any way possible that they could to get me, you know what I am saying, to, um, slow down."

Let me stop you, what you are going to have to do is, at some point, you are going to have to make up in your own mind that you gotta' give up that street life. That's, that's the only way that you are prob- ably going to be able to proceed. Just say, "I can't go back to that." And… we were talking about that yesterday in that… there are four things people have to have in their life. You have to have food. You have got to have shelter. You have to have clothing. And you have got to have security. You have got to be able to feel safe. If you don't have those four things, it ain't going to work. If you don't have food, you've got big problems. If you don't have clothing, you've got big problems. If you don't have shelter, you have got big problems. And if you don't have security, you are going to have big problems. When you are in the street, when you are in that environment that you are talking about, you don't have security. So you are feeling paranoid about your personal safety. And that's what security means, is not feeling paranoid about your personal safety. Now the flip side of that is your parents, when you were in the house not taking your medicine, they were paranoid about their personal safety because of the way they saw that you were acting. So they were like, "We can't have a good life because we have food and we have clothes and we may have shelter, but we don't have security. Because we got our son over here who is acting out and playing street games, bringing it home to the house." Right? "And he won't take his medicine. And we are afraid."

And you can't live very well for very long if you are always afraid. And if you are in a situation where, you know, "I've got this natural paranoia where I don't want to take the medicines because in the environment that I come from I'm going to get hurt if I take the medicines," well, the environment that you are from isn't safe anyway, if that's how people have to handle themselves. You have got to come into your own mind and make a decision that you are going to leave that all behind you. That you are not going to do that street life anymore. And the problem with that is part of it is seductive. Part of it is like... alluring... you want to do it. Because parts of it are fun, parts are exciting. But, and I'm saying this as honestly as I can, that before you can proceed in your life you are going to have to be, "I can't do that anymore. I have got to leave all of that behind. I have got to lead a new life." Or you are going to be stuck where you are. You know, I'm not saying, I'm not talking about being stuck here, but you will be in and out doing the same kind of thing, in and out of jail, in and out of treatment until you get to the point where you decide, "I'm not going to do that kind of life anymore."

Ralph: "Or it will kill you."

Yeah, yeah, think about what I'm, you know... don't be mad at me. I'm just being honest. Because you've got to have, everybody has got to have food, clothing, shelter and safety. And as long as you are putting yourself in an environment that you are not safe, you are going to have trouble.

Demarcus: "Well, you see my neighborhood is like, I'm saying, everybody there knows each other, you know what I am saying, we got our own little group that protects... we don't do nothing violent around the kids... in the neighborhood. We might sit back and drink a beer or smoke a blunt, you know what I am saying... um, listen to the movie, watch a DVD or something like that and just chill, you know what I am saying... we just sit around and talk. Like I'll be the main one talking, but I'm the head man, everybody listens to me. You know what I'm saying, we just be chillin."

How are you going to give that up?

Demarcus: "Huh?"

How are you going to give that up?

Demarcus: "I can't give it up, because... I'm so deep into it that there is only one way out."

No. You just don't go back to that situation. Where are you from? Where are you from?

Demarcus: "I'm from New York, but..."

Where is the neighborhood that you are talking about?

Demarcus: "Rock Hill."

So you don't go back to Rock Hill; you go somewhere else.

Demarcus: "The organization that I am a part of, they have people everywhere you go."

End of group

The previous discussion is of interest on many levels. First, the patients are at different levels of denial and acceptance. Demarcus is still trying to negotiate at this point in his treatment to go back to his previous life. Later in his treatment, he begins to release that past life and thinks about his future and what he needs to do to make it a good one.

Also discussed were four things that all people need to live well: adequate food; clothing; shelter; and safety.

Safety is often overlooked or not thought about correctly. Demarcus made his home unsafe for his parents when he stopped taking his meds. This is the kind of behavior that burns bridges with families. They still love their family member, but they become afraid for their safety. They get worn out.

And the previous discussion talked about the concepts of convergence and being congruent, although those terms were not used. If your behavior conforms to community standards, which is the term used in the group discussion, your behavior will be convergent with society's rules. Your behavior, if convergent with community standards, will also be congruent (in line) with your goal of staying out.

Divergent.
Divergence or divergent behavior is what leads to the idea of "dangerous to themselves or others." How?

There is a phrase that I like: "Perception is reality." Perception is a word that means how people see the world. Their perception of the world is the only reality they can know. But obviously everyone sees things differently, so everyone has their own perception of reality. None of our perceptions of reality are the actual reality. Only God could see all, know all, be all. Human beings, people, just know the reality that they can perceive. Someone who is deaf will have a very different reality compared to someone who is blind. And those two people's reality will be so divergent from each other that they may not be able to communicate at all. Certainly communicating their reality to the other person would be difficult. How would a blind person talk to someone who is deaf? How would a deaf person communicate with a person who was blind?

So our perception of reality is our reality but it is not "the reality."
When someone becomes mentally ill, their reality begins to diverge from the reality that most people perceive. A mentally ill person is considered dangerous to themselves or others when the mentally ill person's reality becomes so divergent from everyone else's perception of reality that other people cannot understand the mentally ill person's behavior. That is when the mentally ill person comes to the attention of society.

So when we say, "make our behavior match our goal," we are also trying to keep our behavior from diverging from the accepted norm. Remember at the beginning we used the example of people yelling and screaming at a football game when their team scores. That behavior is acceptable. But if someone starts screaming in the middle of the street for no easily seen reason, that behavior could be divergent enough to get someone committed to the hospital.

So, to review:

Goal 1. Get Out.

Goal 2. Stay Out.

How?
Make your behavior match your goal.

Frustration:
Have a plan to deal with frustration so that frustration will lead to Social Cooperation and not Social Confrontation.

Don't isolate yourself and develop a support system that includes peer support.

Beware of Takers pretending to be Givers/Receivers.

Be in the Right Place at the Right Time.

Allow others to help you.

The four needs: adequate food, clothing, shelter, and safety.

7   *Getting out: where will you live?*

There are four possible living placements for mentally ill persons with which I am personally familiar. There is a fifth level that I am not familiar with and that is living homeless on the street. I will discuss the four I know. I will call them levels 1, 2, 3 and 4.

Level 1: Inpatient placement

This is the in-hospital placement. Some persons that come into the hospital will require longer-term treatment. They will be moved from an acute-care setting to a chronic-care setting. There are several reasons for this move. The main reason is because there are always new patients that need treatment so space must be made for new patients so patients who need longer-term treatment will be moved to a chronic, long-term treatment setting.

Hopefully, these longer-term treatment areas will have groups that will teach skills for living, but due to budget cuts these settings have become basically holding placements where patients wait for placement in Level 2 settings.

Level 1 settings have little-to-no freedom of movement, although many patients will earn yard cards where they can go out on the hospital grounds during certain times of the day. Otherwise, inpatient settings are characterized by little-to-no freedom with little-to-no responsibility. You are told when to eat, when to bathe, when to take your medicines and when to go to bed. You do not have to worry about food, clothing, shelter and safety. Staff will come and get you to take you to any appointments. There will be staff that make sure the living areas are kept clean.

Level 2: The Group Home
Group homes usually have a little more freedom, along with shared responsibility. Some group homes will do the cooking and cleaning for the residents, but many group home residents will have shared chores. In group homes that have shared chores, the chores will change every week, every two weeks or monthly.

I think this model of changing shared chores is a good model. Over time it will teach each resident the skills they need to keep their own apartment. They will learn how to cook, wash dishes, clean the bathroom, wash clothes and generally straighten up the living area.

In some group homes, residents will have to take care of their own medications, but most group homes will have staff that will give out medicines at the correct time. The staff will also make sure refills of medicines are filled on time. Also, the group home staff will take residents to the mental health center for follow-up appointments. The staff will take residents out to shop at least weekly and they will have other planned trips such as going out to eat or to the movies.

Some group homes will let residents sign out for the day to go to jobs. These group homes are more like so-called halfway houses that are meant to help residents transition to living more independently. The more freedom a resident has, the more the resident is expected to be responsible for taking care of his or her own needs.

Level 3: Assisted living

Assisted living tends to group similar types of people into apartment home situations. For example, there are lots of elderly retirement villages that use this model. There will be planned activities, but each resident will have their own apartment and can do their own cooking if they like and keep their apartment pretty much as they like and they can ask for help when they need it. The assisted-living facility staff will have transportation to take residents to their doctor's appointments and there will also be planned trips into the community.

Assisted living for the mentally ill offers much of the same services as assisted living for the elderly. The elderly resident and the mentally ill resident often share similar needs. Both often have chronic illnesses which require them to take daily medicines and have regular doctor visits. Both have to usually keep and take their medications on their own. Both will use daily medication dosage boxes to organize their medicines for the week or for the month. Sometimes they will organize the boxes on their own, but often a nurse or family member or another staff person will help them organize their medicines. For the mentally ill resident, the mental health center staff will often set up the resident's dosage boxes on their follow-up appointments at the mental health center.

Assisted living allows the residents to live virtually on their own if they like, but help is there when needed. Mentally ill persons living in assisted living will often have part-time jobs. Government work rules will usually only allow people receiving government help for disabilities to work part time. Many mentally ill persons living in assisted living receive some money for disability from the government. This can limit their ability to work.

Living with your family is a kind of assisted-living arrangement. They can help you manage your medications and your money. They can help make sure you get to your appointments. And they can help you plan your leisure time.

Level 4: Living on your own
Living on your own means all the freedom and all the responsibilities. You have to choose a place to live. You have to plan your meals and get your food and cook. You have to get your medicines and take the right dose at the right time.

Often people will have roommates to share the costs of rent and utilities such as heat, lights and telephone service. Sometimes the stresses of living on your own can overwhelm a person so you have to be careful to not take on too much responsibility. For example, cellphones, cable TV and Internet are nice, but how will you pay for those services? While they are nice to have, you do not have to have them. Be careful not to take on too much.

We are all different from each other. So a living placement that is good for one person might have too little freedom or too much responsibility for another person. The more freedom of choice someone has, the more that person will be expected to be able to make good decisions. That is why some people need the help that living in a group home can provide. The more responsibility someone can handle, the more that person will tend to live more on his or her own. But one must remember that the more freedom you have, the more responsibility you will also have. If you live on your own, you have to shop, get to your appointments, get your medications and choose what you are going to do that day, and these responsibilities can be too much for many people to deal with, including people who are not diagnosed with mental illness. Persons with serious mental illness often live in places where they can get help with day-to-day tasks of daily living and that's okay. You want to find a place to live where you can feel good about what you are doing and it is hard to feel good about what you are doing if you feel overwhelmed. So when you get out of the hospital, don't take on too much at one time. Add an activity, one at a time, and see how you are able to deal with the activity before adding another.

8   Medications

Just as no one placement situation will work for everyone, no one medication works for all people. A medication that one person likes might cause side effects in another person. So patients will often be tried on different medication to find the right balance that causes the lowest possible side effects. Older medications that have been around for more than 20 years will often be much less expensive than newer medications, so cost will sometimes be a factor in medication choice.

It is important to know what medicines you are taking and the doses and when you are supposed to take them. You should ask the nurse to write down this information for you so you can learn it. The more you know about the medicines you are taking and why you are taking them, the more empowered or in control you will feel.

When starting a medicine, it is a good idea to write down how you feel while you are taking the medicine, both good feelings and any side effects you may be having. If you write this information down, you can take that information to your follow-up appointment. That is valuable information for your prescriber to know to be able to make changes for your care. You should volunteer information about medicines that you think have done a good job for you in the past, especially if you are seeing a new provider.

Never stop taking your medication on your own. If you don't like a medicine, write down what you don't like about it and take that information with you to your appointment. I say to write it down so that you can remember to share this information during your appointment. It is always best to make notes to take with you to remember questions you want to ask your provider. Most of us, when we go to doctor's appointments, will forget to bring up things we want to ask if we don't have those questions written down. If you are scared to ask on your own, take someone who can help explain your questions or concerns.

Lecture: Stigma of mental illness

There is a wide range of normal behavior or what is considered to be normal behavior because there is no one normal person. You don't pick out one person and say, "Well, that person's behavior is normal," because if you had one person that had normal behavior, everyone else would have abnormal behavior. So there is actually a wide range of acceptable behavior. That's the good news.

The bad news is because you have been in a place like a psychiatric hospital people are eyeing your behavior more closely than they would somebody else. Such as, if a cop gets called in to talk to you, "Oh, you've been down to Columbia," and "Oh, you've been to…"

Nathan, a patient, made the statement that if somebody has been in a psychiatric hospital, they are not taken as seriously by the authorities as someone who has not been in a psychiatric hospital. I think it is a very true statement. He said that if you tell somebody that somebody has deliberately stepped on your foot and hurt you, they go and ask the person that stepped on your foot, "Why did you step on that guy's foot?"

But then, if they find out that you have been in a place like a psychiatric hospital and you have been a mental patient, they, instead of going and asking the person that stepped on your foot, they come back to you and say, "Are you sure that they stepped on your foot or is that just something you thought they did?" So you don't get, you don't get the benefit of the doubt that other people might get?

Julie: "Did that happen to Nathan?"

No, no, that is just an example that he made up. I have no idea what happened with Nathan.

Barry: "There is a stigma attached."

If you want to call "stigma," well, yeah, but what happens is they know your behavior in the past has been not within this range [points to the board range of normal behavior] and it's a wide range of what normal behavior is and they know, or they assume that they know, that the reason you went outside of whatever these boundaries were was because you were misinterpreting or misreading the environment. You thought things were occurring that weren't actually happening and you acted inappropriately on those beliefs. And you did something, usually based on fear, usually based on fear for personal safety but you know every story is different.

Alright, so we want to get out and we want to stay out. We want to make our behavior match our goal. The good news is that there is a wide range of normal behavior. The bad news is that people are looking closely, like, you get out of the mental hospital and you go to a boarding home, there is going to be an increased amount of stress because there is going to be an increased amount of respon-sibilities. And there will be whatever stress that is involved with having however many people in the boarding home that you don't know. Probably, you might know one or two of them, but you will not know most of them and they all have their own issues, so it's your issues rubbing up against their issues, which can create stress. And within that, most boarding homes will have responsibilities that you have to take care of or you get in trouble. People accuse you of stuff, "Did you take my book?" "Did you take my soda?" "Did you take my cookie? You better not take my cookie?!"

[Group laughs.]

So you have all this stuff, and always when you have one of these kind of situations where you have a group of people, some of these people might not be the nicest people in the world. Sometimes you might not be the nicest person in the world. People in boarding home situations can get bored like people anywhere can get bored. And what do they say about boredom?

Several patients say: "Leads to trouble."

Leads to trouble.

Daniel: "The devil's playground."

"Idle hands are the devil's playground"… so boredom leads to mischief. "I'm bored, so let's do something…" and it's a natural tendency 'cause people like to have a certain amount of stimulation. Alright…

So the thing that I would suggest people do is: every day, when you get up, write down your goal for the day. Then make sure your goal for the day matches your goals for where you want to be in the future. Make your behavior match your goal. Figure out what is your goal. If I asked you today what is your number one goal, you would probably say "Get out." Is that close to your number one goal?

Daniel: "It's not my long-term goal."

What's your long term goal?

Daniel: "Staying out."

Staying out.

Curt J.: "And I'm never coming back."

Okay, but to stay out you first have to get out.

Curt J.: "And I'm never coming back."

So you need to ask yourself every day, how do I make my behavior match my goal?

What am I going to do today to make my behavior match my goal? People get trapped in the moment. You know, they argue with other people, they fuss with other people, you know, they get hung up over this, hung up over that...

Daniel: "I mean you know they give you a chance... they give you a chance, um, to rely on what you should do. You should have a normal behavior so, if you allow yourself to do these things, if you realize you have to do things too. But if the normal thing... you have to match your behavior whereever you go."

Right, right. Well, you have to make your behavior match your goal. You also have, I think what you are saying, you have to match your behavior, but you also have to make your behavior fit whatever situation you are in. Like if you stand up and scream and yell... well, you can do that some places. If you are at a football game you can stand up and scream and yell. If you are at a basketball game, you can stand up and scream and yell. You go out to the middle of the street and you scream and yell, they are going to come get ya'.

Right? So you have to recognize the situation that you are in...

Curt J.: "Baseball game, you can stand up and yell."

Think about what situation you are in and "How do I fit my behavior within whatever this wide range of behavior is...?" Okay... and it's really kind of a simple thing if you can do that. Let me match my behavior to the situation that I am in. Alright.

The easiest time for people to lose sight of this goal is when they are angry. They get angry, they get frustrated. And the problem with matching your behavior to your goal all of the time of staying out is there will be times that you are right to be angry. Somebody has treated you wrong. You are justifiably frustrated. And the thing that will make people most angry in my experience is when it is somebody you can't really do anything to... or anything about. That it is somebody that is in a power position above you. And people that go into a boarding home have lots of people that are in power positions above them. You got the staff, you got the mental health center, you got cops, you got... just about anybody you interact with is in a power-up position above you. If one of those people treats you bad... they don't have to be fair, right? Because they are in a power position. People in power positions are only fair because they choose to be. People in power positions only have to be fair through their own sense of ethics; through their own codes of honor. Right?

James: "They might be fair to one person, but might not be fair to the next person."

That's exactly right. People get treated unequally. And that will make people mad, especially people that have mental illness because they don't it. Some people are not going to get, "Why some people get the benefit of the doubt when I don't?" "Why do they get to go when I've got to stay?" "Why do they get this but I get that?" And it doesn't seem fair and sometimes it isn't fair. Sometimes it's just because their situations are different...

Alright, when you are frustrated... that's the hardest time, especially when you are justifiably frustrated, that's the hardest time to match your goal because you have got hot anger. "And I ain't gonna' take it anymore," you know you get that feeling. And what will happen is when people get in that situation, that's when they are most likely to do something that is going to hurt themselves and go against this goal of staying out. Some people, you know, if they have a history of drug abuse, they will say, "Screw it!" and they will go down the street and get themselves a beer... call up old friends, get whatever their drug of choice was... because, "Damnit, I'm pissed off and I'm not going to take it anymore." And they use and they are found out… and they come straight back.

The person that got hurt was themselves.

Daniel: "That is exactly what happened to me. I just got frustrated with the situation, the job situation, saying, like they say in AA, some people get upset when they don't have money. I'm like that. Understand I don't have to have a lot of money, but I like to have money. If I have an emergency, I'm able to take care of that situation. I don't like to be stuck."

Yeah. No, it's frustrating; it's scary. It makes you feel bad about yourself if you are in a situation where you don't have the money, you know, you got to go out ask people…

Daniel: "That's what I mean. I can do, if I'm taking care of myself… and got a job… earning my own keep… but it bothers me when I have to, you know 'cause I can separate myself from other people, specially if I have, know they have certain ways that they look at me and they don't really want to be with me unless I can do something for them anyway, they done proved it over a period of time, so I separate myself from them, then there might be a situation where I have to go ask them for something 'cause you know I really don't want to… you the last person they really gonna' help anyway."

Right, right. Well… this is… the reason I like this model is because it is simple. You know, it's really really simple. You make your behavior match your goal, the big enemy is frustration so you have got to have a plan of how to deal with that frustration BEFORE it happens. Because the one thing that we do know is it's going to happen, right? We all get pissed off. We all get angry. You know there are always things that happen in our lives that don't go our way, you know it may not even be, we just woke up on the wrong side of the bed. It's okay to wake up on the wrong side of the bed.

Everybody does it. You know we all have days where it's just a crappy day.

Daniel: "I had a couple of days like that, where I didn't feel like myself and then I have to go to work and I'm on the way to work, and I'm, like, "Ah, man, I don't feel like this is going to be a good day." You know what I'm saying?"

Yeah. So you gotta' have a way to deal with it. Now the way that I think… the best way to deal with this frustration, is not to try to get rid of it, not try to suppress it, not try to sit on it and not ignore it. Talk about it with somebody. And… but what you want to do is find somebody with whom you can safely talk about your frustration with. Now that could be a staff person, but likely the safest person you are going to find is a peer. Somebody who has also been in the system. People who have been in the same situation are going to understand it, probably better than anybody else. What you are doing by talking with somebody like that is you are trying to have your frustration acknowledged. You do not have to use a peer relationship to get your frustration acknowledged. The relationship could be your mom, your brother, your sister, your aunt, your uncle, a staff person that you get along with really well that gets you… it doesn't have to be peer-to-peer but someone with whom you can express your frustration. Have somebody who will say, "Yeah, I know you are frustrated and, yeah, I see why." Because just having that acknowledgment will allow this frustration to vent enough so that you don't explode on somebody. Because when you explode on somebody, that's a behavior that is not going to match your goal.

So that's the other thing, when you have a confrontation with somebody, so when you have this frustration what you want it to do is lead to social cooperation and not social confrontation.

Daniel: "That's what I can't stand is that social confrontation. I got some people on my side of the family… they still use me drinking and stuff like that…"

Curt J.: "They don't see what happened to you."

Daniel: "I don't understand. I don't want them to feel sorry for me or anything like that, but they don't see things from the point of view that I see because, you know what I'm saying, I'm trying to better myself… and the first thing they say is, 'Well, he can't drink and he can't do this and that, he got a mental problem,' you know what I am saying… I can do what I want to do. And they feel like they are better than you. They say, 'There is a limit to what he can do, I'm doing my thing and that's his problem if he needs something,' you know what I am saying?

Especially if they are under the influence of alcohol, no telling what they thinking or drugs. The first thing they gonna' do is reject me. I got sisters and stuff, I took care of them all my life and I took care of some of her kids… you what I saying 'cause I'm oldest of the family and, um… my daddy went to prison when I was in the ninth or eighth grade and, um, he died about five or six years after he got out of prison so I always had to be the head, take care my family and I got married and I still had to take care of my family. So… I mean, I mean, seem like they don't realize maybe it's time to give something back, you know, all my time, all my years, you know, even my baby brother, I told my baby brother, um, I say, man, you don't realize I'm locked up and he owe me like $10,000. I'm, like, um… man, you don't realize there is a lot of things I do for you. You know what he told me? 'That's what you are supposed to do, you're the oldest brother.' I don't think that was fair at all. I didn't have to do nothing I did; you know, what I'm saying, choose to do that."

Curt J.: " My little brother was talking about my mother the other day and she asked him to come see me with her… so he could see me and, uh, with her. And he went through the fucking roof."

Let's try not to drop the F-bomb. [Class laughs.]

Curt J.: "I didn't mean the F-word but everybody has heard it before. He said it could never be forgiven what I did, that I screwed up to the big time. That I, I, when I got the house, set fire to the house, the dogs and the cat died, and those were his dogs and his cat. He loved them more than me. Plus, he didn't want to split the will with me like was ordered by my daddy. And I need my half of the money to survive on, to get my medicine on, to pay my hospital bills like this place or any other mental health facility that I get sent to in the state for help and try to pay the bill on it. When I get out and get my medication and a place to stay.

Well, we've been in here a little more than 30 minutes, so let's just kind of go back through this:

Goal one, goal two; get out, stay out. You want your behavior to match your goal. You have got to have a plan to deal with the anger or the frustration that you are going to have. I mean, everybody gets frustrated dealing with people sometimes. It's natural. But you want to have a plan in place of how you are going to deal with that frustration so that even when you are frustrated… and angry… that you can maintain your behavior within this normal range so that your behavior continues to match your goal of staying out. If you can do that… if you can do that, if you can do that one thing… manage your behavior when you are frustrated and still keep it working for you so you can stay out… you got it. You got it. I mean that's it, if you can do that you are home free. Home free.

Thank you.

End of group

9   *The Donut Tree*

Why did I name this book The Donut Tree? I named it The Donut Tree in honor of the group where I first had the idea of writing a book. This group was about nutrition and each day I would draw a donut tree on the board at the beginning of the group.

After a while the patients started drawing the donut tree and we applauded each other's art. The point of the donut tree is that there is no donut tree. Donuts don't grow on trees. So what's the point of that?

Well, we will have to back up a little, say ten thousand to 20 thousand years ago, to the cave man days and the days of the hunter/gatherers. Back then, people ate what they could find or hunt. So all of our food came from trees, vines, plants, roots and whatever meat we could hunt. These people would not find this food and save it to put on a plate so they could eat three or four things all at once. They would eat a little where they found the food and save a little for later if there was enough to save. All we have to do now to find food is go through the drive-through at the local fast-food restaurant.

So back to the donut tree. We have two really bad nutritional problems today. The first is the over-abundance of sweets. In nature, fruits and berries are sweet. They are quick energy foods, but they also have lots of vitamins and fiber. It was good for a hunter/gatherer to have fruits for the energy to hunt and gather protein. So we like things that taste sweet. This works against us today, because the only work we have to do to hunt food is to go through the drive-through.

The other problem we have today is that we have too many salty or sweet carbohydrates. These would include potato chips and candy bars… all those things in paper wrappers that you eat and a few minutes later you want another one. The reason we get hungry again so quickly when we eat those snacks is because our bodies break those snacks down extremely quickly so our blood sugar goes up fast, then comes down fast.

Because we don't use that sudden release of sugar energy to do any work, our body will "save" that energy for later. Where does our body store that energy? In fat. So we store the energy from those potato chips or candy bars in fat and, at the same time, feel hungry again! You will hear people talk about empty calories and these bad snacks are what they are talking about.

Probably the worst empty-calorie food is donuts! That's why I started out the group by drawing a donut tree. Now I do eat a donut or two every two weeks and even then it is not good for me but they are fun.

How to Avoid Bad Snacks.
Take a piece of paper or have someone write it for you. Write down the name of your favorite Bad Snack. Draw a line under the name of the snack. Spelling is not important. Then, under the name of that bad snack, make a list of the snack foods that you would eat instead of your favorite Bad Snack.

Possible choices might come from this list:

Blueberries	Kiwi
Strawberries	Apples
Blackberries	Oranges
Watermelon	Peanuts
Cantaloupe	Pumpkin pie
Honeydew melons	Blueberry pie
Dates	Apple pie
Raisins	Walnuts
Grapes	Pecans

You can make your own list.

Shopping for food:

Most grocery stores that I have been in seem to have the same basic arrangement: fresh foods and foods that can go bad quickly are displayed on the outside wall. Usually you walk in and go to the right, and you will see the produce section with fresh fruits and vegetables, then further back you will come to the dairy section or the meat section and, if the store has a deli, it will also be located on the outside aisle as will be the pharmacy if the store has one.

On the inside aisles you will find products that last longer — canned goods and things packaged in boxes.

Somewhere will be frozen foods. Somewhere will be quick-prepare foods that can be microwaved or quickly heated, requiring little work. Also in the frozen food section will be frozen vegetables and fruits.

So what to buy?

Generally speaking, it is better to buy foods on the outside aisle, as these will be your fresh meats and vegetables and fruits. These foods will take longer to prepare, but are better for us. Why?

Foods that are made to be sold in boxes have to have a longer shelf life than fresh foods. To have a longer shelf life, they have chemicals added to make them last and to make them taste good when eaten. Those additives give back the taste that those foods lose from not being fresh. Sadly, those additives, even though they taste good, are not as good for us as fresh foods. That is because they have lots of added fats and salt. So people who live on boxed foods tend to weigh more and have higher blood pressure than people who eat fresh foods.

I should mention that vegetables and fruits that are frozen when they are fresh retain almost all of their nutrient value and I find it convenient to always have fresh frozen vegetables in the freezer. Also, research is starting to show that brightly colored fruits such as watermelon and brightly colored vegetables such as squash, broccoli and carrots can lower our blood pressure and protect us from cancer. The pigments that give fruits and vegetables their color seem to have strong protective benefits. Also cooked tomatoes — in spaghetti sauce or with other pastas — have lots of health benefits.

I heard someone say that the best foods for us are foods that will easily rot, which makes sense. We want to eat foods that our bodies find easy to break down. If a food can fall under the sofa and be found a year later and it looks about the same as when it fell, it is probably not the best food for us to eat from a health standpoint.

The main exception that I can think of are various nuts, including walnuts and pecans and various seeds such as sunflower seeds and pumpkin seeds. Nuts and seeds are very healthy and they last a long time. Still, I would not eat a peanut that had been under the sofa for a year!

10   Three great supplements

Omega-3 Fatty Acid

Melatonin

N-acetyl cysteine

The above three nutrients are all safe and cost very little. All three combined can be bought for about a cost of 20 dollars or less per month. In my opinion, all persons with any type of mental illness should take all three. Also anyone who is concerned about delaying the aging of their brains and protecting both their heart and their liver should take all three, I take them myself.

So what do they do? Remember: there is no donut tree. Eat things that can be plucked from a vine or a tree, or is a root (such as carrots, potatoes and peanuts), or could be hunted or fished.

Omega-3 fatty acid

In the food that we eat, there are three kinds of fatty acids: Omega-3; Omega-6; and Omega-9. Omega-3 tends to be anti-inflammatory, while Omega-6 tends to promote inflammation and Omega-9 tends to be more neutral, neither promoting nor reducing inflammation in the body.

So what is inflammation? A dramatic example would be the swelling produced by a bee sting. The bee stings someone and around the sting wound the body releases chemicals to cause the skin and other tissues to swell so the chemicals in the bee sting can't move into other areas. Inflammation is protective when we are stung by a bee.

But overall tendencies in the body for inflammation are bad. Inflammation leads to heart disease and other problems by causing our blood vessels to narrow, making it harder for our heart to pump blood. Our bodies as a system have a balance between anti-inflammatory and pro-inflammatory tendencies. So how does Omega-3 fatty acid help? First, some brief history.

Up until about 10,000 years ago, most human beings on our planet were hunter/gatherers. That means they lived in small groups that would move around and eat whatever fruits or nuts or roots (such as potatoes, peanuts, carrots, turnips and radishes to name a few) and vegetables that were ripe, and they would try to hunt or fish for meat to eat. And human beings had lived like this for at least 150,000 years, so generation after generation we adapted to that diet. In fact, up until 400 years ago, this was the type of diet that most humans still ate. Then modern industry and changes in farming started to change the way we eat. The way we eat now even has a popular name: it's called the "Western Diet." The Western Diet is named for the diet changes that started perhaps 1,000 years ago in Spain, France, England and other countries considered to be Western Europe. Persons of Western European descent or roots actually have less problem with diseases such as heart disease and diabetes because their families have adapted to the diet over time. They too, however, will also benefit from taking Omega-3 fatty acids. Why?

Having already stated that Omega-9 fatty acid is neutral; neither promoting nor reducing inflammation in the body; Omega-3 decreases inflammation; and Omega-6 increases the tendency for inflammation; what is the point? The point is fatty acid balance. The hunter/gatherer had a fatty acid balance of 2 to 1 or 3 to 1 Omega-6 to Omega-3. For every two or three molecules of Omega-6 fatty acid, the hunter/gatherer took in one molecule of Omega-3. So for 150,000 years we had a balance of 3:1 or 2:1 Omega-6 to Omega-3.

But the Western Diet most of us eat now has a balance of 15 or more of Omega-6 to one molecule of Omega-3. The Western Diet is an inflammatory-promoting diet which tends to make our blood vessels become too narrow, promoting heart disease and other health problems. So by taking Omega-3 fatty acid supplements, we can restore and return our body's fatty acid balance to hunter/gatherer levels.

It has also been found that persons who have problems with their mood, so-called mood instability, get better when their fatty acid balance is restored to hunter/gatherer levels. Your Omega-3 supplements should have both EPA (eicosapentaenoic) and DHA (docusahexaenoic) fatty acids. You can find their mix by looking at the ingredient label. The most common Omega-3 fatty acid supplements are fish oil supplements. Some people complain of after-taste right after taking the supplements, especially if they burp. A good trick I learned is that you can put your fish oil in the freezer and take them frozen. Three or four per day will get you into a much better Omega-3/Omega-6 balance. There is a prescription version of fish oil, but the over-the-counter supplements are fine. If you want your prescription drug plan to pay for your fish oil/Omega-3, ask your medical provider to prescribe it for you.

So the benefits of taking Omega-3 fatty acids include greatly lowering your risk of heart disease and improving your mood stability.

Drawbacks: Tastes bad if you burp right after taking it. Solution to drawback: Get enteric-coated fish oil gel capsules or freeze the gel capsules. They will not thaw until after entering your intestine. When you burp, you can sometimes taste your stomach contents, but not what is in your small intestine. Some people say they can "smell" the fish oil when they sweat. If you have this problem, reduce the number of gel capsules you take daily (from 4 to 3 or from 3 to 2) or try a different brand.

Some foods high in Omega-3: pecans, walnuts, peanuts, various berries, fish and shellfish, including crab, rice bran (cooking) oil.

Avoid using corn-based cooking oil or vegetable oil for cooking as these are very high in Omega-6. Use either rice bran oil, which is available at Asian food markets or olive oil which is very high in Omega-9.

Omega-3 fatty acid comes in 1000–1200 milligram gel capsules and the usual dose is 3 or 4 gel capsules each day.

Melatonin
About half of all patients with serious mental illness will

remember that, before they got sick, their sleep went bad. They could not sleep through the night; they woke up too late or too early. Sometimes they would go more than two or three days without wanting sleep or they did not feel rested when they did get sleep. I always tell people that if your sleep starts to "go bad," you need to let someone know because it is a bad sign when your sleep starts to go bad. That is because not being able to get good sleep is a sign of possible relapse. We have to get good sleep to stay in good balance, both mentally and physically. Any person, mentally ill or not, will start to hear things and start to misjudge cues in the environment if they are not allowed to sleep for a week or more. That is why deliberately not letting someone sleep is a form of torture sometimes used in wartime.

Our body makes hormones that keep us alert during the day, but these same hormones that keep us up put stress on the body. Sleep lets us dump those stress hormones. We have other hormones that build up while we are awake that, as they build up, make us want to rest. Drugs such as caffeine and other stimulants such as nicotine, cocaine and amphetamines block the action of the hormones that make us want to get rest. So we should not drink caffeine within five hours of going to sleep or smoke cigarettes right before going to bed. And, of course, we should not be using cocaine or other illegal drugs at all. Mental illnesses can also block our ability to sleep and, sadly, the longer we go without sleep, the more divergent our thinking becomes.

So why melatonin? Our brain has internal timing controls that tell us when we should be awake and when we should be asleep.

Melatonin actually allows us to reset that internal clock. The problem is that, as we age, our brain makes less and less melatonin so everyone's sleep, mental illness or not, tends to get more and more unregulated as we age. I like to explain how melatonin works like this:

Have you seen how kids, before they reach 10 or 11 years of age, can play all day but then, when they go to sleep, they are out? You can pick them up, move them around and they never wake up. That's because their brains make really high levels of melatonin. But when they reach 10 or 11, those levels start to drop really fast and that signals the body to go into puberty, when they start to become young men and women. That's why teenagers have such a hard time with their sleep. By the time most people reach their early 20s, they get used to the lower levels of melatonin and they start sleeping through the night again, but our levels continue to drop as we age. This is why people in their 70s and above start to have such a hard time sleeping through the night.

Persons with mental illness have it even worse. Recent studies have shown persons with mental illness have problems with the genes that maintain the correct timing of their internal clocks which is probably why their pre-illness problems start to show up usually during their teens or early 20s, after their melatonin levels have dropped. The good news is that melatonin can be bought over-the-counter in the United States and it is both safe and cheap! But for best results it must be used correctly and often the labels do not tell you the best way to take it or the labels even tell you the wrong way to take it! So how to take it and how much?

First, melatonin is really short-acting and is easily overpowered by things such as caffeine. So you do not want to use any stimulant medications hours before you want to go to sleep. If you smoke, you should not smoke after taking melatonin. Second, melatonin does not make you have to go to sleep like strong sleep medicines. You can wake up if you need to. The main mistake that people make when taking melatonin is that they take it like a sleep drug. They will take it 45 minutes to an hour before they go to sleep. They will say, "I felt sleepy about 20 minutes after I took it but, when I tried to go to bed, I couldn't go to sleep." Exactly right. I like to think of it like a surfer catching a wave. You have to catch the wave before it has gone past. They felt sleepy about 20 minutes after they took it, but waited before going to bed so they missed the wave. So to catch the wave you want to take it about 20 minutes before you want to go to sleep.

Melatonin is a natural hormone, so it is metabolized (or processed) very quickly. It's gone an hour after you take it. So how does it work? It starts your normal sleep stages; it just kicks off those normal stages. So there is no early morning hangover. The only main side effect it has is that you will have better dreams! What it also does is set your internal alarm clock or sleep clock. You can actually set the time you want to go to sleep the next day! For example, say you want to go to sleep every day at about 10 p.m. Take your melatonin 20 minutes before you want to go to sleep. Go to bed. Even if you don't get to sleep right away the first night, you have set your sleep clock for 10 p.m. the next night. The next night, take melatonin 20 minutes before and you have again set your clock for 10 p.m. the next night. Every time you take it at the same time, you are resetting the clock for the next night. It will work.

Part of normal sleep is that sometimes we do wake up in the middle of the night. Because melatonin is so short-acting, as long as you have 2 to 3 or more hours that you can sleep, you can retake it. Some people when they retake melatonin in the middle of the night say they can see little flashes of light right before they fall asleep. This is normal and happens because the part of the brain where melatonin works is also associated with vision.

So, how much to take? Melatonin is sold in various doses, with the smallest dose being 3mg. As with any substance, you want to take the smallest amount possible at first just so you have confidence you are okay taking it. After trying 3mg, go up to 6mg. If you can only find 5mg at your store, you can start with that. Usually 6mg or 9mg works with most people. I currently take 15mg a night and I have taken as much as 25mg a night. But I really enjoy the dreams. Some cancer doctors will have their patients take really large doses because melatonin is also a very good anti-oxidant and can lessen the side effects of cancer treatments.

One of the other benefits of melatonin is that it signals your body to dump the byproducts of stress hormones that build up during the day. I had a patient once who was having dialysis treatments because her kidneys had totally failed, so three times a week she had to be hooked up to a machine to clean her blood. She was very stressed and said she always felt both tired and anxious, and even though the strong sleep medication she had been prescribed in the past made her sleep, she still felt tired when she woke up. I told her about melatonin and the next time I saw her she thanked me over and over, and asked why no one had ever told her about melatonin. And I said because it is over-the-counter, most providers don't know much about it because they have never been taught about it or how it should be given. Anyway, within a few weeks, with my approval, she weaned herself off her other sleep meds and is doing much better now.

Which brings me to my next point. You can take melatonin with any other sleep medication you are taking without any problems. Melatonin is very soft-acting and is a natural hormone. Until you reached puberty, your brain used to make lots of melatonin. Melatonin will not interfere or interact with other sleep meds or any other medicine you are taking. But it will still signal your body to dump the daily byproducts of your stress hormones so you will feel more rested. Before you stop taking other sleep meds, tell your provider you want to try melatonin. I say this because some medicines that people take for sleep also have antipsychotic actions, so never stop taking a medication on your own because that would not be congruent or in line with your goal of staying out of the hospital.

About where you sleep: some people watch TV in their bedroom. If you are in a boarding home, you probably do lots of things in your room besides just sleep. If possible, the only thing you should do in your bedroom is sleep and have sex. This is because the more behaviors you have associated with your bedroom, the harder it is to get into the right mindset to go to sleep. Do not watch TV while you are in bed. You will fall asleep, but then something will happen on the TV and you will wake up. And believe it or not, part of you monitors the TV while you are sleeping so you hurt your deep sleep by having a TV going while you are sleeping. Try to have your bedroom cool and dark. If you need to have a night light so that you can get up to go to the restroom, make sure you cannot see it directly from any spot while lying on your bed in a sleeping position. This is because, even though you might go to sleep not looking at the light, we all roll over while we sleep and having the light directly in your eyes could wake you up. These little ideas are part of what people call "good sleep hygiene."

A side note: I was once the sole medical provider for 34 chronically mentally ill state hospital patients. I started two patients at a time on melatonin and slowly withdrew all of the patients' sleep meds. All of the patients said they slept better than they could remember. The nursing staff also reported everyone seemed to be sleeping better. Because everyone was getting better rest, we had fewer problems with behavioral outbursts than any other lodge at the place where I worked and this was documented by the hospital's own statistical records. So melatonin WORKS! If your sleep is good, you will be good.

Melatonin: Start with 3mg 20 minutes before bedtime. Try to keep the same bedtime each night. The usual effective dose is 5 to 15mg 20 minutes before bedtime. You may retake half of your nightly dose if you wake up and still have 2 to 3 or more hours that you can sleep.

N-acetyl cysteine

How I learned about N-acetyl cysteine is an interesting story. I have long searched dietary articles to find nutrients that would protect the brains of persons with schizophrenia and bipolar disorder. But I stumbled on N-acetyl cysteine while looking for something else. I mentioned before that I'm a big guy. I'm almost

6'5" and weigh about 220 pounds. As a kid, because I was bigger than other kids my age, I had to work hard to not be clumsy at sports. Big kids tend to be more clumsy than their smaller classmates because the big kids have to grow more nervous tissue. Like wiring up a house for electricity, a bigger house will need more wiring than a smaller house. My son is a REALLY big kid. At the time I am writing this, he is 12-and-a-half years of age and is 5'10" tall (almost 6'!) and weighs 181 pounds. He's huge. When he reaches full adult height, he will be at least 6'6" tall and will likely weigh at least 240 pounds. I tease him sometimes that I'm going to sell him to the NFL (National Football League). Anyway, because I am tall and his mom is tall, and because I had to work hard to be coordinated, he has played sports since he was 5 years old, starting with kids' soccer, then baseball. Now he is interested in baseball, basketball and football. I had been looking for a nutrient to add to help him develop his nervous tissue as quickly as possible. I already had him taking Omega-3 fatty acid supplements. When he started talking about wanting to play football I, of course, started to worry about how to protect him from head injury.

So while looking for a nutrient to add to Omega-3 fatty acid to help him develop his nervous system and protect him from possible head injury or concussions from playing football, I found N-acetyl cysteine. And the more I read, the more I was amazed that N-acetyl cysteine is not always given to persons in chronic danger of head injury such as football players or people with brain diseases such as schizophrenia or bipolar disorder or depression. I'm amazed it is not given to persons suffering from brain injury due to trauma, such as soldiers or stroke victims as a basic first-line part of treatment. And it's CHEAP. Six dollars or less will buy more than a month's supply if you take 1200mg a day. Besides its effects on the brain, it also removes heavy metals from your nervous tissue and empowers your liver to do its work of cleaning your blood.

One of the neat things about our body is that our body will use the same chemical to do different things in different parts of the body. N-acetyl cysteine is the raw ingredient that our bodies need to make glutathione. Glutathione is probably the most important chemical you can affect by nutritional supplements. The more you have, the better off you are and the easiest way to increase it is to take N-acetyl cysteine supplements, which converts directly into glutathione.

So more about what N-acetyl cysteine (which becomes glutathione) does…

First, the brain. In our brain we have thinking cells called neurons. Also we have cells whose job is to take care of the neurons and make sure they are healthy. These helper cells are called glial cells and they use glutathione to do their work. Persons with schizophrenia and bipolar disorder and, to a lesser extent, depression have less glutathione available for the glial cells to do their job, so persons with those mental illnesses have neuron cell death that other people don't experience. This is important. Persons with severe mental illness are at high risk to lose their ability to think because they don't have enough glutathione to maintain the health of their neurons. This is NOT a good thing. But it can be avoided by taking N-acetyl cysteine which has been shown by itself to improve the symptoms of schizophrenia by at least 20 percent.

Also, stroke victims who are given N-acetyl cysteine have up to a 40 percent reduction in permanent brain damage as compared to those who do not receive N-acetyl cysteine. It is this fact that leads me to believe all football players should take N-acetyl cysteine to protect them against concussion. I also think all soldiers should be taking N-acetyl cysteine to protect themselves from the brain injuries that occur from the shock of explosions common in warfare.

Our liver and N-acetyl cysteine
Glutathione is needed by the liver to do its work of detoxifying chemicals that might otherwise hurt our system. Many medicines are processed by the liver, including Tylenol. When people overdose on Tylenol, emergency rooms will give the patient N-acetyl cysteine, which is then converted to glutathione. The glutathione both protects the liver and allows it to process the overdose. Without the N-acetyl cysteine, a Tylenol overdose can use up all the patient's glutathione, potentially destroying the liver which can lead to the death of the patient. Glutathione is required by the liver to do its work.

N-acetyl cysteine is also very safe. Another effect it has is thinning the mucous in the lungs of people with serious lung problems such as cystic fibrosis. People who have cystic fibrosis are "medically fragile," which means they are very weak physically and can't handle much stress or side effects from medicines or nutrients. But N-acetyl cysteine is safe for these medically fragile people to take.

Benefits of N-acetyl cysteine:
1. At least a 20% reduction in the symptoms of schizophrenia.
2. Protects the neurons of persons with depression, schizo-phrenia and bipolar disorder.
3. Reduces damage caused by stroke by as much as 40%
4. Protects the liver from damage by toxins, while at the same time allows the liver to process those toxins.
5. Likely protects brains from impact trauma, both short-term and long-term.
6. Helps to thin mucous and is used by seriously ill patients with lung disease.
7. Removes heavy metals, including lead and mercury, from our nervous systems.

Glutathione levels in our brains get lower as we age. Taking N-acetyl cysteine can increase our levels of glutathione and, therefore, hope-fully slow the aging of our brain by keeping our neurons healthy.

The dose is 600mg to 1200mg a day. It comes in 600mg capsules. People allergic to sulfa drugs can take it.

So to review the three nutrients and their doses:

Omega-3 fatty acid. Comes in gel caps of 1000 to 1200mg each. Be sure to get a good mix of EPA and DHA fatty acids. Take 3 to 4 gel caps a day. You can freeze them so you don't taste them if you burp right after taking them.

Melatonin: Start with a low dose (3mg) but aim for a dose of 5 to 15mg nightly. Take it 20 minutes before you want to go to sleep (catch the wave like a surfer) and try to go to sleep about the same time each night as every time you take it you are setting your internal clock for the next night. If you wake up and have 2 to 3 hours left that you can sleep, you can take half your normal dose and go back to bed. You might notice little flashes of light even with your eyes closed right before you go to sleep again. This is normal.

N-acetyl cysteine (also called NAC). Take 600 to 1200mg daily. It usually comes in 600mg capsules.

11   The Last Group

So everybody knows who we were just talking about right? They got caught with marijuana. Has anybody noticed that his mood has been different for the last week or two?

Charlie: "Yeah, he almost got in a fight or two."

Umhm. So even though this is health styles, let's assume his first goal was to get out. Did that behavior help…? He flunked. That behavior of smoking pot didn't help, did it?

Charlie: "No."

If he did that when he got out it wouldn't match his goal of…

Curt J.: "Staying out."

Yeah. And then the question becomes, "How in the heck did he get it?" That's not for me to worry about, but that is an interesting question isn't it?

Curt J.: "If we could answer that, we could answer all the questions around here."

Um, alright, so let's talk about it from the aspect of body…

Curt J.: "Mind and spirit."

Yep. Alright, definitely, we are here in a mental hospital.

Curt J.: "Yeah, we know that."

Well, it's a prison, a special kind of a prison, it is what it is, might as well call it what it is. The medications that people take here for their mind [points to triangle on board with the words mind/body/ spirit at each point] they are drugs that are supposed to affect your mind; are they perfect?

Curt J.: "No."

They are not perfect.

Curt J.: "We are not perfect people."

Well, they are not perfect anyway.

Curt J.: "They were not designed in a perfect way... for the brain."

Well, they are not precise enough.

Curt J.: "The brain is an unknown field."

[Charlie laughs...]

Now what he is saying is partly correct. But what, my point is these drugs are not perfect and I would be lying if I said they were and I am not going to sit here and lie to you because what's the point of that? You'd know that I was lying. All they are to do, all they are really meant to do, is to help people control their behavior in such a way that they can match their goal of getting out and staying out. These drugs are not perfect. They will be better 10 years from now. They will be better 20 years from now. There is a very cool thing that is going on in medicine right now... who here has heard of DNA? [Group affirms they have all heard of DNA.]

Curt J.: "It's the molecule of the body made up of strands."

Yeah, yeah, it's a double helix. They just got through, not too long ago, with mapping all the DNA of human beings. As everybody knows, some people are tall, some people are short, some people have dark skin, some people have light skin, some people have blue eyes, some people have brown eyes... we have all these little genetic differences. A medicine that might be good for him [points to a patient] might not be good for you [points to another patient]. Right, just because of genetic differences. Okay, like you can't take Haldol. He might like Haldol. Right? Might do him well, but it doesn't do you good at all. Right? Alright, that is because of genetic differences.

Charlie: "Haldol doesn't do me well."

There's another person. So what will happen is, drugs get more advanced and, as science gets more advanced, we will be able to come and say we are going to have a blood test. The blood test will tell us what drugs work well for you, but right now it is kind of hit-and-miss, and that is why people get tried on one medicine and, if that doesn't agree with them, they get tried on another medicine. One of the things that I have always asked patients is, "Are there any medicines that you have taken in the past that you thought worked really well for you?" Each person in here should remember individually for himself or herself, as you are put on medicines, if there is a medicine that you think, "Hey! This is a good medicine for me. Not only was I able to think well, I was able to function well and I felt comfortable in my own skin while I was taking that medicine." It is in your own, personal best interest.

Remember what that medicine is, write it down. Even though they have certain protocols here using intramuscular monthly dose typical [Haldol and Prolixin Decanoate] anti-psychotic meds as first-line medicines in this forensic psychiatric hospital, when you get out you will be able to go to your practitioner and say, "Hey, when I was... you know the best drug I ever took for me was drug X," whatever drug X is. And they will say, "Really? So you really liked that?" Prescribers should work with you because people will take medicines that they like taking; they will say, "Okay, let's try that."

Curt J.: "They were giving me Risperdal, and then they put Haldol with it and took the Risperdal away and increased the Haldol. I don't shake anymore."

Okay, well, good, I've seen that you don't shake anymore. They started you on a beta blocker too, didn't they? [Beta blockers can help stop tremors.]

Well, Inderal is a really good pill for hand shaking.

Toby: "I'm doing really well with my medicine since they started giving me a green pill. But it makes me sleepy."

Well, find out what medicines you are on. One of the things that people do, what Toby just did is he said, "They are giving me a pill that is this color." Right? The problem is there are lots of drug companies, make lots of different kinds of pills. And once a drug goes "generic," whereas you had a brand... brand-name drug products are made by the company that developed them. And they get so many years to sell that product by themselves, nobody else can make that drug so the drug company that developed it can get paid back for their research. But then after their drug goes off-patent, generic companies can start making it...

Lawrence: "So they can change the color of the pills..."

So they can change the color, they can change it to whatever they want. So when you say, "Well, I was taking a yellow pill...," well, that doesn't really mean anything. You need to know what the name of the chemical is or the name of the drug is... you are taking Vasotec, right?

Cassie: "Yeah."

Okay, that's a blood pressure medicine. I take Vasotec, too.

Devonte: "Yeah, but when you in the medicine line and you see you are missing a medicine you can say, 'Well, I'm missing the green one or whatever color it is.'"

Right, right, yeah, that's good because you are getting the same thing over and over again…

Charlie: "I had a lady in there that was new and I started counting and I had six medicines and only should have had five."

Yeah, Devonte did a good job correcting me on the idea that, when you are in medication line, if you see that a pill isn't there or if you see a pill you have never seen before, you should stop and ask, "What's that?" or "Why isn't such-and-such in there?" So that's a good point.

But, like, she knows that she is taking Vasotec and I know because I am taking Vasotec, well, what we are actually taking is a chemical called "enalapril," which is the generic name of it…

Cassie: "What is it called?)

Enalapril; Vasotec is enalapril. Each drug has two names. Like for Vasotec, Vasotec is the brand name and enalapril is the generic name, okay? So when I call up my pharmacist to get my prescription refilled, I usually say, "I need to get my enalapril." Just because I know the name, okay? Now the point is, if you ask for "Vasotec," you are asking for the brand name but because it's generic now you are probably not getting Vasotec the brand; you are probably getting enalapril the generic because it's cheaper.

Cassie: "My Vasotec is blue."

Where you say yours are blue, mine are orange. They are both enalapril, the coloring is just food coloring.

Lawrence: "It's the same thing. It's just a different color."

Yeah, it's the same thing; it's just a different color because it's made by a different company. So it's good to know if there is a medicine that does well for you, but don't say, "The green pill does really well for me" or "The blue pills do really good for me." Be able to say, "Well, Vasotec does a good job of controlling my blood pressure..." if it does, right? And I think you are taking Norvasc too, right? [Cassie nods yes.] And HCTZ. So you would say these three medicines are doing a good job... like if you were to change prescribers and they would ask, "Well, what were you taking for your blood pressure?" And you would say, "Well, I was taking Vasotec and I was taking Norvasc and I was taking HCTZ and they were doing a good job." Same thing with mental health medicine. Like Lawrence here can't take Haldol. I mean, it doesn't kill him if he takes it; he just doesn't feel good if he takes it. Jeff here is, like, "I am fine with it." Curt over there, he is fine with it. So each person is different what they tolerate. Right?

Charlie: "I just don't like it because makes me feel bad."

That's a perfectly good reason not to be taking it. "I don't feel good when I take it. I'm antisocial when I take it." Would you keep taking a medicine that makes you feel bad?

Lawrence: "A lot of times the doctor will go along with about your medication if you talk with him and see. A lot of times he will change if he knows that the medicine be doing what it is doing 'cause he knows some of the side effects of the medicine and, if it's bad for you, he will change that."

Cassie: "I'm taking about 15 different medicines and I don't know which ones are good and which ones are bad."

Well, the first thing for you to do is think back, if you can, to all the way when you first started taking medicines.

Cassie: "I can't remember, though."

Well, you need to start thinking about it though, because if you think about things, the way the brain works, the way your memory works… everybody here has had the sensation of like, "What was that word? I can't remember what that word was." You know you are looking for a word to describe something and it is at the tip of your tongue, you know it's, like, "Gah, I just had it a minute ago and I can't remember what the word is." And you go on and you can't remember it and then, "Oh, I remember!" Right? Well, it's the same thing, once you start thinking about, "What, well, was it and what was it doing?" Well, you can't remember it right this minute, but if you think about it and start going over it, you will build back the neurons to pull it up and you will remember it. I mean, you won't remember all of it, but you will remember a lot of it, you will remember a lot more than you can remember right now. And you just think about the associations, "Where was I? What was I doing? What was going on? Who was there?" You know, those kind of associations about anything you want to remember — you start thinking about the context of what the memory occurred in to pull up what it was… so I would encourage everybody, you know, "Of all the medicines that I have ever taken, which ones do I think did a really good job?"

Now getting back to him, using marijuana on these kind of meds, his mood changed. I mean, I was, like, I had no idea what was going on with him. Did you see his mood change?

Charlie: "He got a red band and 6-months' restriction."

Lawrence: "He got a red band and 6-months' restriction?"

Charlie: "Yeah. He can go outside but he just can't go to the cook-outs."

That's bad.

Alright, well...

Dan: "He should have just waited until he got out."

Well, but where will that have led?

Dan: "Coming right back in here."

Yep.

Curt J.: "What we are doing by taking our medicine, we are working toward getting out and staying out. And we are experimenting with the drugs to make sure we are on the right medication and to get out."

Devon: "I just want a cigarette and a diet soda." [Class laughs.]

I hear ya'.

Curt J.: "How about a regular soda?

Hey, you know why I drink diet soda? You drink diet sodas, you can eat more candy bars. [Class laughs.]

Thank you, thank you, be here all week, try the veal.

Cassie: "If you got put on restriction 6 months, you got to wait a year to a green band, but you got to get a yellow band first."

Curt J.: "I've had this green band for four or five years."

Danny: "When you max out, what are they going to do, take you to court or something?"

Uh, I don't know all the legal stuff. I do know people have been discharged as yellow bands.

Lawrence: "The red bands, they will go back to jail."

Cassie: "Do they discharge you to a community care home when you get out?"

I don't know. It's different for each person. It just matters what your situation is, you know, that gets back talking about this stuff, we haven't talked about this in a while. A forensic mental hospital is a place where you have very little freedom or no freedom. You go to a group home, you have a little more freedom, but you also have a little more what?

Curt J.: "Restriction."

Dan: "Responsibility."

Responsibility. More freedom, but more responsibility. Then you can go to an assisted-living apartment which has more freedom and more responsibility. And you can go to total freedom which has more freedom but also has much more responsibility. And this level might not be good for everybody. Huh?

Charlie: "I was told by my treatment team that I would be going home."

Okay, well, that will be good. You will be here [indicates total freedom/total responsibility]. But the problem is if you mess up here [indicates boarding home], you come back here [forensic mental hospital]. If you mess up here [points to assisted-living apartment], you come back here [points to forensic mental hospital] and if you mess up here [points to living on your own] you come back here [points to forensic mental hospital]. So the problem is, or the thing to keep in mind, some people would be more comfortable staying in the group setting where they have a little bit more freedom, a little bit more responsibility. Some people are going to need more freedom, they say, "Man, I'm going to need more freedom than that." But they have to realize with that freedom, and that's what gets people in trouble, is they don't think about with the freedom comes the responsibility. Right? If you deal with the responsibility well, either this [points to assisted-living apartment] or that [points to living on your own] would be good. I think that would be fine as

*long as you make sure your behavior matches your goal of
staying out.*

Lawrence: "Be where you need to be."

*Be where you are supposed to be when you are supposed to be. Yes.
So, anyway, we got a little sidetracked today by what happened.
That will do it unless someone has any questions?*

End of group

You have to learn to manage your own behavior or other people
are going to be managing it for you.

Afterword

I dedicate this book to my friend Doug, Doug and I were good
friends in high school.

Our senior year in high school, Doug disappeared for about six
weeks. When he got back, he told everyone he had been visiting
his family in the Caribbean (The Islands), but it was weird. Later
he showed me a paper he was very proud of and I read it. I loved
Doug but it made NO sense. Doug had schizophrenia, but I didn't
know what it was at that time. Doug had not been in "The Islands";
he had actually been at Hall Institute in Columbia, South Caro-
lina, where kids and teenagers with mental illness were treated.

After getting out of high school, I went to Doug's house several
times a year for two or three years, but Doug was never there and
his family always said he was in Washington, D.C. What I did not

realize then was that he was in a hospital somewhere. I miss my friend and would do anything to have him back as he was or at least as the best that he could be.

I hope you will work hard to be the best you can be. I'm pulling for you and your family.

May your behavior match your goal.